BREAKING THE CHAINS OF SELF-SACRIFICE

A Guide to Reclaiming Your Worth and Ending Toxic Relationships

Stella Joseph

Dedication

To the brave souls who have dared to regain their peace, who have had the courage to break free from toxicity, and who have chosen to put their own well-being first.

Contents

Introduction

The air was thick with unsaid tension, like a real weight bearing down on my chest. A familiar tightness clutched my throat as I sat across from him, my partner, the guy I loved. However, at that moment, love seemed like a faraway memory, a faded echo of what once was. His remarks, harsh and accusing, penetrated the veneer of normality we had painstakingly built. I could feel the familiar sting of tears welling up in my eyes, and a burning flush of embarrassment rising up my neck. This wasn't the first time, and it would not be the last.

I was locked in an age-old waltz of emotional manipulation and silent pain. The screenplay was always the same: his rage, my tears, his apology, and my forgiveness. Rinse, repeat. I convinced myself it was simply a hard time, that he was stressed, and that the terrible things he said were unintentional. But, deep down, I knew I was lying to myself.

I was drowning in a sea of self-doubt and remorse, my soul deteriorating with each passing day. I wanted to break away from this poisonous cycle, to recover my voice and authority, but the fear of upsetting the boat, of losing him, held me immobilized. I was stuck in a web of contradictory emotions, divided between my feelings for him and the gnawing anger in my spirit.

Then came the turning point, a seemingly trivial event that altered the course of my life. We were at a dinner party with friends when he made a snarky comment about my looks, a poorly veiled attack masquerading as a joke. I could feel the familiar sting of embarrassment, the need to withdraw into myself and vanish. But this time, something inside me broke.

"Enough," I heard myself utter, my voice barely a whisper at first but becoming louder with each word. "I'm not going to tolerate this anymore."

The room became quiet, with everyone's gaze riveted on me. My partner's face distorted, expressing astonishment and rage. But I held firm, my voice steadfast as I informed him that I deserved to be treated with dignity, and that his statements were offensive and unacceptable.

Something inside of me altered at that moment. A spark of resistance kindled, along with a glimmer of optimism that I may be able to break out from this poisonous relationship. It was not easy. There were tears, disagreements, and restless nights filled with self-doubt. But I stood steadfast, believing that I deserved better.

Saying "enough" triggered a sequence of profound transformations in my life. It was more than simply terminating a bad relationship; it was about recovering my authority, voice, and self-esteem. It was about learning how to establish boundaries, prioritize my own needs, and surround myself with people that encourage and support me.

I realized I'd spent years repressing my own voice for fear of upsetting or failing others. However, in the process, I lost touch with my genuine self, interests, and aspirations. Saying "enough" was the first step in rediscovering my own identity and what I wanted out of life.

Chapter 1: The Silent Scream Within

The pain in your chest is a regular companion, a slow throb that worsens whenever they are close. You tell yourself it's work-related stress or a lingering cold, but you know it's something more. This uneasiness, this chronic disquiet, is your soul's silent cry when locked in a poisonous relationship.

I remember my previous self. The vivacious, outgoing lady who always smiled in the face of adversity. When I started dating Mark, my light began to fade. My laughing grew less frequent, my eyes lost their gleam, and my once-confident stride became tentative. Friends saw the shift, but I dismissed it with excuses. "He's just going through a tough time," she'd explain, or "It's my fault, I'm being too sensitive."

However, as the months passed, the signals grew more difficult to ignore. Mark's subtle put-downs disguised as jokes harmed my self-esteem. His continual craving for attention left me feeling exhausted and unloved. The vivacious lady was gradually receding into the background, her voice muted by the weight of his expectations.

My tale is not exceptional. Toxic relationships are deceptive, frequently masquerading as love and compassion. They infiltrate our lives, leaving a path of emotional devastation in their wake. The tiny indications are easy to overlook, particularly in the beginning when we are blinded by passion or optimism. But as time passes, the faults in the veneer grow increasingly visible.

Perhaps you've seen a pattern of belittlement in which your spouse discreetly diminishes your accomplishments or rejects your emotions. Perhaps they separate you from friends and family, making you feel as if you are the only one who fully understands them. Perhaps they control you via guilt trips and emotional blackmail, making you feel responsible for their happiness.

These apparently little acts of emotional abuse may have disastrous repercussions over time. According to research, continuous stress, such as that experienced in a toxic relationship, may cause a variety of physical and mental health issues. Depression, anxiety, high blood pressure, heart disease, and even autoimmune illnesses have been linked to the harmful consequences of chronic stress.

Furthermore, toxic relationships may undermine our self-esteem and leave us feeling helpless and confined. We may begin to believe the bad things our spouse says about us, internalizing their critiques and questioning our own capabilities. This lack of self-belief may have far-reaching consequences, affecting everything from our employment to our relationships with others.

So how can you know if you're in a toxic relationship? Begin by listening into your instincts. That nagging sensation in your belly is more than simply indigestion; it's your body's warning flag. Pay attention to how you feel when you're with your spouse. Are you feeling elevated and invigorated, or exhausted and depleted? Are you feeling comfortable and secure, or worried and on edge?

If your relationship is bringing you more grief than pleasure, it's time to reconsider your options. Consider the questions below:

- Is your spouse regularly criticizing or belittling you?
- Do they attempt to regulate your conduct or separate you from loved ones?
- Do you feel nervous around them, scared to offend them?
- Do they make you feel guilty or responsible for their feelings?
- Do you regularly make excuses for their behavior?

If you responded yes to any of these questions, you should get treatment. Contact a trustworthy friend, family member, therapist, or support group. Know that you are not alone, and there is no shame in asking for assistance.

Identifying the Signs of a Toxic Relationship

In the shadows of your relationship, subtle signals may indicate a harmful undertone. Does your spouse gradually undermine your confidence with backhanded comments or "jokes" that hurt too much? Do they reject your sentiments or make you feel bad about expressing them? Perhaps they isolate you from friends and family, creating an environment in which their voice is the only one you hear. Perhaps they influence you with guilt or fury, leading you to doubt your own sanity.

These are not separate episodes; rather, they form part of a larger pattern of emotional manipulation and control. Recognizing these signals is the first step in recovering your power and declaring "enough."

The Hidden Costs to Your Mental, Emotional, and Physical Health

A toxic relationship's impact on your well-being is typically subtle, sneaking into every aspect of your life like a quiet poison. While the emotional wounds are frequently the most evident, the effects on your mental and physical health may be as severe.

Under Mark's influence, I, once a beacon of optimism, transformed into a shell of my former self. My exuberant vitality faded, replaced by chronic tiredness and a pervasive feeling of dread. I couldn't focus at work, my sleep was disrupted by nightmares, and I lost my appetite. My body was screaming for assistance, but I blamed my symptoms on stress or a fleeting sickness, unconscious of the underlying cause of my pain.

Many people who are caught in toxic relationships suffer from a variety of mental and physical problems. Constant stress and mental instability may cause or worsen anxiety and depression, leaving you feeling overwhelmed, helpless, and detached from yourself. The weight of the relationship might appear as physical discomfort, migraines, digestive issues, or even a compromised immune system, making you more prone to sickness.

The subtle nature of these interactions might make it difficult to draw the dots between your decreasing health and the toxins you're experiencing. You may blame yourself, believing that you are just not strong enough to face life's obstacles. However, toxic relationships are like slow-burning flames that consume your energy and vitality until you feel empty and shattered.

If you are suffering any of the following symptoms, it is important to explore the influence that your relationship may be playing in your health.

- Persistent fatigue and low energy levels
- Difficulty sleeping or frequent nightmares

- Changes in appetite or weight

- Increased anxiety, worry, or panic attacks

- Feelings of sadness, hopelessness, or worthlessness

- Loss of interest in previously enjoyed activities

- Physical symptoms such as headaches, stomachaches, or muscle tension

- Weakened immune system and frequent illness.

Recognizing the link between your health and relationship is the first step toward recovery. Recognizing the hidden cost to your well-being allows you to make empowered choices that prioritize your health and pleasure.

Self-Reflection Questions:

1. Do you feel like you're dimming your light for your partner? Have you observed any changes in your self-esteem, confidence, or general happiness since starting this relationship?

2. Does your partner's conduct leave you feeling exhausted, nervous, or on edge?

3. Do you feel isolated from loved ones, or does your spouse discourage you from connecting with friends and family?

4. Do you feel guilty or blamed for things that are not your fault in a relationship?

5. Do you often defend your partner's conduct to yourself or others, even if it seems wrong?

Transformative Exercises:

1. Diary for Awareness: Keep a diary to express your emotions and experiences in the relationship. Write openly about your feelings, both joyful and unpleasant, without passing judgment. Observe any reoccurring patterns or themes that develop.

Transformative Exercise: Diary for Awareness

Objective: To enhance self-awareness and understanding of emotions and experiences within the context of your relationship.

Instructions:

1. **Create a Dedicated Space:**

   - Choose a journal or digital platform where you will consistently write. Ensure it's a place where you feel comfortable and secure expressing your thoughts.

2. **Set a Regular Writing Schedule:**

   - Aim to write in your diary daily or at least several times a week. Consistency is key to uncovering patterns and gaining deeper insights.

3. **Write Freely and Honestly:**

- Express your emotions and experiences without censoring yourself. Let your thoughts flow naturally, whether they are positive, negative, or neutral. Avoid self-judgment during this process.

4. **Reflect on Specific Experiences:**

- Describe specific incidents or interactions that stood out to you. Detail your feelings, thoughts, and reactions in these moments.

5. **Identify and Explore Patterns:**

- After a week or two, review your entries. Look for recurring themes or patterns in your emotions and experiences. Pay attention to any repeated situations that trigger similar feelings.

6. **Pose Reflective Questions:**

As you review your diary, ask yourself questions to deepen your understanding:

- What emotions do I feel most frequently in this relationship?
- Are there specific triggers for my positive or negative emotions?
- How do I typically respond to challenging situations?

- What patterns can I see in my partner's behavior and my reactions?

7. **Observe Changes Over Time:**

- Notice any shifts in your emotions or perspectives over time. Are there certain times when you feel more connected or distant? What changes in your circumstances or behaviors correspond with these shifts?

8. **Use Your Insights for Growth:**

- Use the patterns and themes you've identified to make informed decisions about your relationship. Consider how you might address recurring issues or enhance positive experiences.
- Reflect on what you've learned about yourself and your needs. How can this awareness guide your actions moving forward?

9. **Celebrate Your Progress:**

- Acknowledge and celebrate any progress you make in understanding and managing your emotions. Recognize that self-awareness is a continuous journey and each step forward is valuable.

Example Entry:

Date: June 12, 2024

Today's Experience: Today, I felt a deep sense of frustration during our conversation about weekend plans. I wanted to spend time together, but my partner seemed disinterested. This left me feeling unimportant and dismissed.

Emotions:

- Frustrated
- Sad
- Unimportant

Thoughts:

- Why doesn't my partner care about spending time with me?
- Am I asking for too much?
- Maybe I'm overreacting.

Patterns:

- This is the third time this month I've felt this way after discussing plans.
- I notice that I often feel unimportant when my partner doesn't show enthusiasm for my suggestions.

Reflection:

- What can I do to communicate my feelings more effectively without feeling confrontational?
- How can I manage my expectations to avoid feeling hurt in these situations?

Action Steps:

- Plan a calm discussion with my partner about how I feel and explore ways we can find a compromise.
- Practice mindfulness techniques to manage my emotional reactions in the moment.

Your Entry: Follow the instructions and example above to fill in your entry.

Puzzle Exercise

Instruction:

Find the hidden words in the puzzle. Words can be written horizontally, vertically, or diagonally, forward or backward. Circle each word you find.

At the end of your attempt, check the Answer table to find out how correct you are.

Patterns of Toxic Relationships

```
        F D A U B N S V Y C V I Q W O
D O F T G H Q Q G D A V W P B O F Q P C E C
Q E N U T S O V V U C H A P P R O V A L L E
Q K E X P E C T A T I O N S L A Y U G M L M
C Z W P A L Z Y F X Q L N H S E M A F G - C
S A C R I F I C E O Y Z T F B L A S A I B O
S L U I Z - K L W Q H H S D L N C S F D E M
B E O W N W Q F P R I O R I T I Z E I E I P
O O S K E O M A U F B M J O B G C R A N N A
P M I G J R A F A I S D I X U M O T M T G S
B C A R E T A K E R S G B O U N D A R I E S
G U G Z H H J Q M A R E S E N T M E N T B I
R R D O D U D Z J E R K W N O K S A E Y D O
A T N E E D S N Z I I V L U P F Z P W Z J N
Q O P O E C Q N E H Q K S G W H G F M M H D
R V G I R E L A T I O N S H I P S I J J E F
U Z O F U M D L Z A J F I S R Y C F X I Y T
B E L I E F S C K R F Y T J W T H D A B V K
```

Abuse	**Partner**
Anxiety	**Relationship**
Confidence	**Sadness**
Emotional	**Self-Esteem**
Fatigue	**Signals**
Feelings	**Spouse**
Guilt	**Stress**
Health	**Toxic**
Manipulation	**Unloved**
Mental	**Well-being**

Chapter 2: The Myth of Self-Sacrifice

The concept of self-sacrifice is deeply established in our cultural fabric, and it is often praised as the pinnacle of love and compassion. We are taught from an early age that putting others' needs before of our own is noble, unselfish, and the highest kind of compassion. But what if this apparently good deed is really a poisonous lie, trapping us in toxic relationships and preventing us from living authentically?

This fallacy is especially prevalent among women, who are generally expected to be caretakers, nurturers, and peacemakers. We are supposed to prioritize the needs of our spouses, children, families, and even friends, often at the risk of our own health. We are taught that our worth comes from our capacity to give, sacrifice, and prioritize others. However, the persistent pursuit of selflessness may deplete our own resources, leaving us feeling empty, bitter, and stuck.

We can take the instance of a lady – let's say Katherine, who devoted her life to her family. She cooked, cleaned, organized, and chauffeured, always prioritizing her husband and children's needs before her own. She seldom made time for herself, feeling that her self-worth was dependent on her capacity to care for others. Katherine's hatred intensified throughout the years, however. She felt invisible, unheard, and underappreciated. Her once-vibrant energy faded, replaced with a smoldering resentment she couldn't articulate.

Katherine's narrative is a cautionary tale about the perils of unrestrained self-sacrifice. When we continuously put other people's demands above our own, we lose our sense of identity, purpose, and pleasure. We become martyrs, giving up our enjoyment on the altar of society demands.

People-pleasing psychology is complicated, with roots generally traced back to childhood events and a strong dread of rejection. We may have learnt that our value is conditional, based on our capacity to satisfy others. We become chameleons, changing our conduct to meet the expectations of others around us. However, this continual shape-shifting makes us feel alienated from our genuine selves, trapped in a labyrinth of other people's needs.

The fear of failing others is a strong incentive, causing us to say yes when we truly want to say no, to accept things we disagree with, and to put our own needs on hold. We are worried that if we do not comply, we will be condemned, rejected, or abandoned. This dread may immobilize us, stopping us from establishing appropriate boundaries and advocating for ourselves.

But what if the answer to liberty is to embrace our right to say enough? What if we could liberate ourselves from the constraints of self-sacrifice and restore our power? The good news is: we can. It begins with knowing that our value is not determined by our capacity to satisfy others. We have intrinsic value just because we are humans.

We must grasp the difference between healthy selflessness and self-destructive sacrifice. There's a distinction between assisting someone in need and always prioritizing their needs above our own. We may be sympathetic and loving while yet prioritizing our own well-being.

Setting limits is critical. We must learn to say no without shame or apologies. We must prioritize our own needs and provide time for things that offer us pleasure and contentment. This does not suggest that we cease caring about others; rather, it implies that we acknowledge that our own well-being is equally vital as theirs.

Overcoming the fear of disappointing others requires bravery and practice. How do you chart this terrain? Learn to recognize the people-pleasing tendencies in your life. What scenarios make you fearful of rejection? What do you fear will happen if you do not comply? Once you've found the patterns, you may begin to confront them. Remind yourself that you have the right to say no, establish boundaries, and prioritize your own needs.

Challenging Social Expectations and Gender Roles

Katherine's tale is far from rare. It's reminiscent of a well-known music that has been performed repeatedly across history and civilizations. Women, in particular, face the weight of cultural standards that promote selflessness as the supreme feminine attribute. We are taught to be the glue that ties families together, emotional anchors for our spouses, and constant sources of comfort and support. While these traits are commendable, the trouble emerges when they become the main measure of our value, obscuring our own wants and goals.

Consider the fairy stories we grew up with. The princesses, who are often presented as paragons of virtue, are honored for their selflessness and constant dedication to others. They face adversity, abandon their aspirations, and even forfeit their lives for the sake of love or duty. While these tales are engaging, they perpetuate a detrimental narrative that associates female value with altruism.

This story goes beyond fairy tales and into our daily lives. Women are often commended for their maternal nature, multitasking skills, and desire to put others first. While these characteristics are important, they should not be the exclusive determinants of our value. We are more than simply caretakers, moms, and spouses; we are multifaceted persons with distinct abilities, interests, and goals.

Challenging cultural expectations and gender norms is critical to our well-being. It entails acknowledging that we have the right to prioritize our own needs, establish boundaries, and follow our aspirations. It entails rejecting the concept that our worth stems entirely from our capacity to help others.

This does not imply that we renounce our loving nature or stop helping those we care about. It simply means striking a good balance between giving and receiving, or altruism and self-preservation. It entails acknowledging that our personal pleasure and well-being are as vital as everyone else's.

By defying conventional conventions and expectations, we pave the road for a more meaningful and honest existence. We overcome the limits of gender roles and realize our full potential as individuals.

We say "enough" to the illusion of self-sacrifice and take back our power, empowering ourselves to live a life that genuinely represents our beliefs and wants.

Unmasking the Risks of People-Pleasing

The temptation of pleasing others is misleading, since it promises approval and belonging. However, beyond this façade lies a perilous road of bitterness, exhaustion, and self-destructive behavior.

Many people-pleasers get locked in a loop of giving while ignoring their own wants and needs. They get so consumed with making others happy that they lose sight of their own pleasure. The continual endeavor to please may be exhausting, both physically and mentally. It's like running a marathon without pausing to rest or refuel.

Unmet wants may breed animosity, poisoning even the most loving relationships. It might seem as passive-aggressiveness, impatience, or a retreat from closeness. The once-harmonious relationship becomes tense, with underlying complaints and a feeling of injustice.

Furthermore, people-pleasing may lead to a loss of identity. When you are continuously molding yourself to meet the expectations of others, you lose sight of your own values, objectives, and aspirations. You become a reflection of others' wishes, rather than a distinct person with your own light to shine.

The hazards of people-pleasing are real and widespread. It's a route that may result in emotional weariness, bitterness, and self-destructive behavior. However, by understanding these threats, you may start to break free from this damaging cycle and recover your ability to say "enough."

Self-Reflection Questions:

1. Do you prioritize others' needs above your own? Consider your relationships, employment, and personal responsibilities. Where do you find yourself saying "yes" when you truly mean "no"?

2. Do you feel guilty or frightened about asserting your demands or setting boundaries? Investigate the source of these sentiments. Are they motivated by prior experiences, cultural standards, or a desire to avoid rejection?

3. Have you ever felt unnoticed, ignored, or underappreciated in relationships? Consider how your desire to impress others may have influenced these sentiments.

4. How do social or cultural norms influence your willingness to prioritize others' needs? Consider the messages you've received on gender roles, family dynamics, and cultural standards.

5. Identify your key principles and non-negotiables. Determine which principles are most important to you and what limits you need to create to safeguard your well-being.

Transformative Exercise:

1. Identify your people-pleasing behaviors: Keep a notebook to record the instances or relationships in which you prioritize the needs of others before your own. Consider the fundamental reasons driving these tendencies.

Transformative Exercise: Identify Your People-Pleasing Behaviors

Instructions:

1. **Set Up Your Notebook**: Dedicate a section of your notebook specifically for this exercise. Title it "People-Pleasing Behaviors."

2. **Daily Recording**: At the end of each day, take a few minutes to reflect on your interactions and record any instances where you prioritized the needs of others over your own.

3. **Analyze and Reflect**: For each entry, consider the fundamental reasons driving your people-pleasing tendencies. Are you seeking approval, avoiding conflict, or

feeling guilty about saying no? Understanding these motivations can help you address and transform these behaviors.

Example Entry:

Date: June 12, 2024

Situation: My colleague asked me to cover her shift at work on short notice.

What I Did: Despite having planned a relaxing evening for myself, I agreed to cover her shift.

Feelings and Thoughts:

- Initially felt frustrated because I had to cancel my plans.

- Felt anxious about her reaction if I said no.

- Felt responsible for her problem.

Underlying Reasons:

- Fear of disappointing others and seeking their approval.

- Avoidance of potential conflict.

- Belief that being helpful equates to being a good person.

Reflection:

- Realize that my need for approval often leads me to neglect my own needs and well-being.

- Understand that setting boundaries is crucial for my mental and emotional health.

- Acknowledge that saying no can be done respectfully and doesn't make me a bad person.

Action Plan:

- Next time, take a moment to evaluate my own needs before responding.

- Practice saying no in a polite but firm manner.

- Remind myself that it's okay to prioritize my own well-being.

Your Entry:

Date:

Situation:

What I Did:

Feelings and Thoughts:

Underlying Reasons:

Reflection:

Action Plan:

Puzzle Exercise

Instruction:

Find the hidden words in the puzzle. Words can be written horizontally, vertically, or diagonally, forward or backward. Circle each word you find.

At the end of your attempt, check the Answer table to find out how correct you are.

Setting Healthy Boundaries

```
            F D A U B N S V Y C V I Q W O
D O F T G H Q Q G D A V W P B O F Q P C E C
Q E N U T S O V V U C H A P P R O V A L L E
Q K E X P E C T A T I O N S L A Y U G M L M
C Z W P A L Z Y F X Q L N H S E M A F G - C
S A C R I F I C E O Y Z T F B L A S A I B O
S L U I Z - K L W Q H H S D L N C S F D E M
B E O W N W Q F P R I O R I T I Z E I E I P
O O S K E O M A U F B M J O B G C R A N N A
P M I G J R A F A I S D I X U M O T M T G S
B C A R E T A K E R S G B O U N D A R I E S
G U G Z H H J Q M A R E S E N T M E N T B I
R R D O D U D Z J E R K W N O K S A E Y D O
A T N E E D S N Z I I V L U P F Z P W Z J N
Q O P O E C Q N E H Q K S G W H G F M M H D
R V G I R E L A T I O N S H I P S I J J E F
U Z O F U M D L Z A J F I S R Y C F X I Y T
B E L I E F S C K R F Y T J W T H D A B V K
```

Approval	Identity
Assert	Needs
Beliefs	Norms
Boundaries	Pleasing
Caretakers	Prioritize
Compassion	Relationships
Conflict	Resentment
Expectations	Sacrifice
Fear	Self-Worth
Guilt	Well-being

Chapter 3: Breaking Free from the Cycle of Guilt

Guilt, like our shadow, often accompanies us through life, whispering doubts and accusations into our ears. It may be an effective motivator, encouraging us to rectify wrongs and make apologies. However, it may also act as a smothering force, locking us in a loop of self-blame and humiliation. To break away from this pattern, we must first recognize the distinction between healthy and poisonous guilt.

Healthy guilt is a gentle push that reminds us of our ideals and duties. It occurs when we have really damaged someone or violated our own moral compass. This form of guilt serves a purpose by encouraging us to apologize, make apologies, and learn from our errors. It allows us to develop and become better versions of ourselves.

Toxic guilt, on the other hand, acts like a heavy chain, weighing us down and keeping us trapped in the past. It is the guilt we experience for things that are not our fault, like establishing boundaries, prioritizing our own needs, or just being human. Toxic guilt is sometimes unreasonable and disproportionate to the circumstances, making us feel worthless and embarrassed.

Assuming you have chosen to quit a poisonous friendship that is draining your energy and happiness. Healthy guilt may drive you to reflect on your part in the friendship and how you may have better conveyed your needs. Toxic guilt, on the other hand, would swamp you with self-blame, making you doubt your choice and feel like a bad person for putting your own well-being first.

To break away from the cycle of guilt, we must learn to identify and address our guilt triggers. Triggers are experiences, ideas, or feelings that cause us to feel guilty. They might be external, like a harsh statement from a loved one, or internal, like a recollection of a previous error.

Keeping a guilt notebook is a very effective practice for recognizing guilt triggers. When you feel a wave of remorse come over you, take a minute to write down the incident, your thoughts, and your feelings. Observe any patterns or repeating themes. Are there individuals, places, or things that constantly make you feel guilty?

Once you have recognized your triggers, you may begin to reframe them.

Reframing is the process of modifying how you see a situation. Rather just taking your guilt at face value, consider if it is genuinely warranted. Is it grounded on facts or illogical beliefs? Are you holding yourself to unreasonable expectations? Are you accepting responsibility for situations that are not your fault?

For example, if you feel bad about saying no to a request that would fill up your calendar, remind yourself that you have the right to establish limits and prioritize your own needs. You're not selfish; you're responsible.

Mindfulness exercises may also assist to alleviate guilt-induced distress. Mindfulness is the practice of paying attention to the present moment without judgment. When you find yourself caught up in guilt-ridden thoughts, take a few deep breaths and concentrate on your senses. What do you perceive, hear, smell, taste, and feel? By focusing on the present moment, you may build distance from your ideas and emotions, enabling you to react to them more effectively.

Another mindfulness approach is to develop self-compassion. This entails treating oneself with love and sympathy, just as you would a friend who is hurting. Instead of beating yourself up over your errors, accept them with compassion and concentrate on learning and developing from them.

Breaking out from the cycle of guilt requires time, effort, and practice. However, by distinguishing between healthy and toxic guilt, recognizing and reframing guilt triggers, and using mindfulness practices, you can recover your power and lead a life free of unneeded self-blame and shame.

Understanding the Roots of Toxic Guilt

The origins of poisonous guilt are often hidden deep inside our prior experiences, influenced by messages we received as children and demands imposed on us. Many of us bear the burden of previous events that have formed our relationship with guilt. Perhaps we were reared in a home where perfection was required and any mistakes were treated with criticism or punishment. Perhaps we were taught that our emotions were a burden to others, so we learnt to repress them in order to avoid generating conflict.

These early experiences might instill a profound notion that our value is based on our capacity to match the expectations of others. We grow fearful of disappointing or offending others around us, which feeds our poisonous guilt.

Understanding the source of our guilt is an important step toward breaking free from its grasp. Recognizing the messages and events that have created our ideas allows us to question them and develop new, empowered narratives. We may learn to distinguish between guilt that benefits us and guilt that hinders us, enabling us to live a truer version of ourselves.

Reframing Guilt as a Force for Change

Instead of considering shame as a burden, what if we regard it as a catalyst for development and transformation? Just as my anger spurred my desire for change, guilt, when used correctly, can be a strong motivator to break away from destructive routines and embrace a life that is consistent with our beliefs.

Consider guilt a warning sign that something is wrong. It serves as a reminder that we have deviated from our intended course, compromised our beliefs, or disregarded our own needs. Rather of repressing or dismissing this signal, we may utilize it to drive change.

When guilt strikes, instead of wallowing in self-blame, ask yourself, "What can I learn from this?" How can I make amends? How can I stop this from occurring again? By framing guilt as a learning opportunity, we change from a victim to an empowered state.

Perhaps you feel terrible for not establishing clear boundaries with a buddy who consistently oversteps. Instead of berating yourself, interpret this shame as a signal that it is time to state your demands and set healthy limits. Perhaps you feel guilty about ignoring your own well-being while caring for others. Use your guilt as motivation to prioritize self-care and lead a more balanced existence.

Guilt may also be an effective tool for personal development. We may learn and grow by recognizing our faults and accepting responsibility for our actions. We may develop more compassion, understanding, and empathy.

Reframing guilt as a motivator for transformation entails changing a bad feeling into a constructive force. It's about harnessing guilt to inspire self-reflection, progress, and, eventually, emancipation.

Self-Reflection Questions:

1. What prior messages and experiences have influenced your relationship with guilt?
2. Can you identify events or people that trigger poisonous guilt?
3. How does guilt affect your body and emotions? What bodily sensations or emotions do you get while you're feeling guilty?
4. What are the negative thoughts that contribute to your guilt? Are you subjecting yourself to high expectations or accepting blame for things that are not your fault?

5. How may guilt be seen as a learning opportunity instead than a source of self-blame and shame?

Transformative Exercises:

1. Keep a notebook to identify your guilt triggers. Write down the scenario, your thoughts, and your feelings whenever you feel guilty. Search for patterns and repeating topics.

Transformative Exercise: Identifying Guilt Triggers

Objective: This exercise aims to help you identify and understand the triggers of your guilt. By keeping a detailed record of situations where you feel guilty, you can begin to recognize patterns and repeating themes, leading to better self-awareness and strategies to manage guilt.

Instructions:

1. **Keep a Notebook**: Dedicate a notebook specifically for this exercise.

2. **Record Guilt-Inducing Scenarios**: Each time you feel guilty, write down the scenario, your thoughts, and your feelings in detail.

3. **Analyze Patterns**: After recording several entries, review them to identify common triggers and recurring themes.

Example Entry

Date: June 12, 2024

Scenario: I skipped my morning workout.

Thoughts: "I should have pushed myself to go to the gym. I'm so lazy and undisciplined. This will set back my progress."

Feelings:

- Guilt

- Frustration

- Disappointment

Analysis: This entry suggests that I feel guilty when I don't adhere to my fitness routine. The recurring thought is that missing a workout equates to laziness and lack of discipline. This indicates that my guilt is tied to a high standard I set for myself regarding exercise and fitness.

Your Entry:

Date:

Scenario:

Thoughts:

Feelings:

Analysis:

Puzzle Exercise

Instruction:

Find the hidden words in the puzzle. Words can be written horizontally, vertically, or diagonally, forward or backward. Circle each word you find.

At the end of your attempt, check the Answer table to find out how correct you are.

Inner Healing and Self-Care

```
              B Z I K F O M L Z I   G O X Y X
  E T B Q J E Y D S R E F R A M E V S Q F K R
  M F O R G I V E N E S S V T R S A A M Y H V
  X I U X R E M O R S E H Q B G Z S R I B O A
  H B N F I X F K Z P A A L G H R F U N W Z D
  P P D W D C W Z Q O I M T A O X W T D I D Q
  C F A D E Q G X O N G E S Z N A N F F D N W
  F G R V N A C C U S A T I O N S C M U S D G
  H P I L T X E E W I C E R D Q P A Q L G P T
  F E E A I I D X L B W E L L - B E I N G R P
  U R S O T X H U M I L I A T I O N R E R I P
  X F A E Y J C S E L F - C O M P A S S I O N
  V E X P E C T A T I O N S F J T J J S P R V
  V C X X Q C F Z N T R I G G E R S P C D I O
  F T W V C Q H F L Y O U C L F Y G U I L T V
  B I J M R Z O C P S X Y U M S C I Y B V I W
  C O M P A S S I O N Z J G D C E E G B V Z L
  K N E J Y D D K E Z C G C F S M S S L M E E
```

<table>
<tr><td>Accusations</td><td>Perfection</td></tr>
<tr><td>Boundaries</td><td>Prioritize</td></tr>
<tr><td>Compassion</td><td>Reframe</td></tr>
<tr><td>Expectations</td><td>Remorse</td></tr>
<tr><td>Forgiveness</td><td>Responsibility</td></tr>
<tr><td>Guilt</td><td>Self-Compassion</td></tr>
<tr><td>Humiliation</td><td>Shame</td></tr>
<tr><td>Identity</td><td>Toxic</td></tr>
<tr><td>Learning</td><td>Triggers</td></tr>
<tr><td>Mindfulness</td><td>Well-being</td></tr>
</table>

Chapter 4: Reclaiming Your Power

Reclaiming your power is a path of self-discovery and self-affirmation, a statement that you will no longer be a passive participant in your own life. It's about removing the layers of society conditioning and embracing your own self, replete with your own values, needs, and wants. This approach starts with establishing your core values and non-negotiables, which are the essential concepts that influence your choices and behaviors.

Take a time to consider what genuinely matters to you. What attributes do you like most about yourself and others? What are you reluctant to compromise on? These might be honesty, integrity, respect, compassion, authenticity, or any other values that speak to your spirit.

Once you've defined your basic principles, it's time to define your non-negotiables. These are the boundaries you create to defend your values and guarantee that your relationships and interactions are consistent with your basic convictions. Non-negotiables might be huge or tiny, like refusing to accept rudeness or denying invites to gatherings that sap your energy.

For example, if honesty is one of your basic values, you may make it a non-negotiable that you will not be in partnerships with individuals who routinely lie or manipulate. If authenticity is essential to you, you can establish a rule that you will not pretend to be someone you are not in order to impress others.

Setting limits is a strong expression of self-love and respect. It means, "This is who I am, and this is what I will not tolerate." It is a proclamation that you value your own well-being and will not let others infringe on your limits.

To establish successful limits, first communicate your wants and expectations clearly and frankly. Do not presume that others understand what you are thinking or feeling. Be explicit about what you need and what you will not tolerate. For instance, rather of stating, "I don't like it when you're late," say "I feel disrespected when you're late, and I would appreciate it if you could be more punctual in the future."

When establishing limits, be prepared for opposition. Some individuals may not like your new limits, particularly if they are used to having their way. It is critical to be solid and consistent, even if it means enduring pain or confrontation. Remember, you are not responsible for how others respond to your limits. You are accountable for your own well-being.

Setting boundaries may be difficult, particularly if you are used to pleasing others or avoiding disagreement. It is normal to feel guilty, frightened, or concerned about offending others. However, keep in mind that your needs are legitimate, and you have the right to self-defense.

Self-affirmation may help you overcome your fear of expressing yourself. Remind yourself that you deserve respect, love, and good relationships. You have the right to say no, establish boundaries, and prioritize your own well-being.

Another effective method is to envision yourself effectively establishing and maintaining your limits. Consider yourself speaking eloquently, standing tall, and being steadfast in your beliefs. This mental rehearsal might make you feel more prepared and powerful while dealing with real-life events.

It's also critical to surround oneself with positive individuals who respect your limits. These might be friends, family, therapists, or support groups. Having a solid support system may provide you the motivation and affirmation you need to be true to yourself.

Reclaiming your power is a journey rather than a destination. It's a continuous journey of self-discovery, acceptance, and assertiveness. By recognizing your values, creating boundaries, and conquering your fears, you can break free from the self-sacrifice cycle and move into your genuine power.

Identifying Your Core Values and Non-negotiables

The quest to restore your power begins with a deep dive into your inner terrain. It's about discovering your essential values, the guiding principles that govern your thoughts, choices, and actions. These beliefs serve as a compass, guiding you toward a more honest and satisfying existence.

Think of your beliefs as non-negotiable elements in your life's cuisine. Just as a baker would not compromise the quality of their wheat or eggs, you should not sacrifice the ideals that define you.

Take a minute to think on the times in your life when you were most connected to yourself, when you had a sense of purpose and pleasure. What ideals were at play in such instances? Perhaps it was honesty, as you told the truth with bravery. Perhaps it was compassion, as you lent a listening ear to a friend in need. Perhaps it was your creativity, which you conveyed via art or music.

Identifying your essential beliefs is a very personalized process. There are no right or incorrect answers. What important is that you pick values that are meaningful to you, values that you are ready to defend and advocate for.

Once you've determined your basic principles, it's time to turn them into non-negotiables. These are the boundaries you create to defend your values and guarantee that your relationships and interactions are consistent with your basic convictions.

For example, if respect is one of your key beliefs, you may make it clear that you will not accept disrespect from anybody, regardless of their connection to you. If authenticity is essential to you, you may establish a rule that you will not pretend to be someone you are not in order to impress others.

Identifying your basic principles and non-negotiables provides a firm platform for recovering your control. You acquire clarity on what is genuinely important to you, and you empower yourself to make decisions that uphold your beliefs and safeguard your well-being.

Setting Healthy Boundaries with Confidence

Setting boundaries isn't about erecting barriers to keep people out; it's about creating a safe and holy place for yourself to grow in. Consider your limits to be a distinct property line that defines where your own space starts and ends. Healthy boundaries safeguard your well-being in the same way that a fence does for a garden, enabling you to thrive without fear of intrusion or violation.

Many of us find it difficult to create and maintain appropriate limits. We may be afraid of rejection, disagreement, or causing others to feel harmed. However, remember that establishing limits is not selfish; it is an act of self-preservation. It's about respecting your ideals, needs, and limitations.

Begin by recognizing the areas of your life that need greater limits. Are you with a spouse that ignores your feelings? A family member that is continually criticizing your decisions? Or a buddy that drains your vitality with their drama? Once you've recognized the areas that need care, it's time to create restrictions.

Maintain straightforward and direct communication. Don't hide your needs or apologize for them. Express your limits calmly and assertively, using "I" phrases to describe how their conduct impacts you. For example, instead of stating, "You always make me feel bad," say, "I am hurt when you speak to me that way."

Remember, you do not have to justify your limits. They are legitimate only because they are yours. If someone disregards your limits, it is not your obligation to persuade them differently. It is their obligation to respect your boundaries, just as you are responsible for respecting theirs.

Enforcing your limits requires boldness and persistence. It may be unpleasant at first, particularly if you are accustomed to pleasing others. But with practice, it will become easier. Remember, you are not responsible for how others respond to your limits. You are accountable for maintaining your own serenity and well-being.

Setting appropriate limits is a kind of self-empowerment. It's about recovering your power and gaining control of your life. Setting clear boundaries creates a secure environment for you to grow, free of the restraints of toxic relationships and destructive routines.

Self-Reflection Questions:

1. Identify the key ideals that govern your life decisions.
2. Can you recall any times when you sacrificed your ideals to appease others?
3. In which areas of your life do you sense the need to set tighter boundaries?
4. What are your worries or anxiety about creating and maintaining boundaries?
5. How would your life change if you constantly followed your principles and non-negotiables?

Transformative Exercises:

1. Value Exploration: Make a list of your main values. Consider why they are important to you and how they affect your life.

Transformative Exercise: Value Exploration

Step-by-Step Guide

1. **Identify Your Main Values**:

   - Take some time to reflect on what matters most to you. Think about what principles guide your decisions and actions. These are your core values.

2. **List Your Values**:

   - Write down a list of your main values. Aim for at least 5-10 values that resonate with you deeply.

3. **Consider Why They Are Important**:

   - For each value, write a brief explanation of why it is important to you. Reflect on how each value influences your thoughts, behaviors, and decisions.

4. **Reflect on How They Affect Your Life**:

- Think about specific examples of how these values have played a role in your life. Consider both positive impacts and any challenges you may face in living according to these values.

Example Entry

Value: Health

Why It's Important:

- Health is fundamental to my ability to enjoy life and perform daily activities. It enables me to be energetic, productive, and resilient.

How It Affects My Life:

- I prioritize regular exercise, balanced nutrition, and adequate sleep. This value influences my daily habits, such as meal planning and scheduling time for physical activities. It also affects my social life, as I prefer activities that promote well-being and avoid those that might be detrimental to my health.

Your Entry:

Value:

Why It's Important:

How It Affects My Life:

Puzzle Exercise

Instruction:

Find the hidden words in the puzzle. Words can be written horizontally, vertically, or diagonally, forward or backward. Circle each word you find.

At the end of your attempt, check the Answer table to find out how correct you are.

Creating Personal Space and Independence

```
            T  J  T  V  T  C  O  N  F  I  D  E  N  C  E
Z  T  W  O  R  T  H  C  V  L  A  R  I  T  Y  A  T  H  K  B  P
A  O  R  E  S  P  E  C  T  R  E  F  L  E  C  T  I  O  N  Z  M  A
K  V  U  G  L  E  R  K  B  D  U  P  S  U  P  P  O  R  T  S  J  S
V  M  F  S  E  L  F  -  D  I  S  C  O  V  E  R  Y  X  D  V  M  S
W  Y  P  V  K  R  -  A  W  O  R  S  C  Q  L  S  O  X  K  K  T  E
N  E  C  R  J  Y  Q  B  I  G  H  K  O  L  Y  W  R  X  S  N  I  R
Q  M  A  K  I  P  E  U  E  W  J  E  M  P  O  W  E  R  M  E  N  T
A  U  T  H  E  N  T  I  C  I  T  Y  P  L  D  D  E  L  K  C  T  I
L  K  Y  T  D  X  C  B  O  U  N  D  A  R  I  E  S  I  N  D  E  V
J  R  E  J  E  C  T  I  O  N  Q  G  S  E  R  E  N  I  T  Y  G  E
L  P  U  A  T  S  B  H  P  Y  K  J  S  X  A  H  M  O  E  E  R  N
C  C  Y  B  W  L  H  Y  Z  L  J  S  I  E  N  G  F  N  J  H  I  E
P  L  K  L  D  N  O  N  -  N  E  G  O  T  I  A  B  L  E  S  T  S
E  L  S  C  M  Y  L  Q  J  D  I  S  N  B  H  R  J  T  J  S  Y  S
S  E  L  F  -  A  F  F  I  R  M  A  T  I  O  N  U  S  R  O  U  W
D  S  N  X  F  Y  T  T  R  Z  U  P  E  J  U  A  N  T  I  A  E  F
Y  V  Z  N  F  S  Q  S  L  P  R  V  Y  U  K  O  L  K  J  O  J  H
```

Assertiveness	Reflection
Authenticity	Rejection
Boundaries	Respect
Clarity	Self-affirmation
Compassion	Self-discovery
Confidence	Serenity
Empowerment	Support
Integrity	Values
Non-negotiables	Well-being
Principles	Worth

Chapter 5: The Art of Assertive Communication

Assertive communication emerges as an elegant but strong partner, enabling us to convey our wants and feelings in an honest and respectful manner. Unlike passive communication, which often leaves us feeling ignored and angry, or aggressive communication, which may ruin relationships and create conflict, assertive communication achieves a delicate balance between valuing ourselves and others.

Consider a situation in which a buddy repeatedly cancels arrangements at the last minute, leaving you unhappy and unappreciated. A passive approach would entail suppressing your emotions and pretending everything is OK, while an aggressive response might involve striking out in rage and accusing them of being thoughtless. However, an aggressive answer might include admitting your dissatisfaction and expressing your need for more dependable communication.

The core of assertive communication is active listening and the use of "I" statements. Active listening is completely concentrating on the speaker, paying attention to their words, tone of voice, and body language. It entails setting aside your own opinions and judgments and genuinely listening to what they have to say. Active listening demonstrates respect and empathy, fostering an environment conducive to open and honest conversation.

"I" comments, on the other hand, are an effective way to convey your emotions and demands without blaming or criticizing the other person. They move the attention away from their conduct and into your own experience, lowering defensiveness and increasing understanding. Instead of stating, "You always interrupt me," you may say, "I feel frustrated when I'm interrupted because it makes me feel like my thoughts aren't valued."

To practice assertive communication, explore the following scripts and role-playing exercises:

- Scenario: Your boyfriend often leaves dirty clothing on the floor.
- Passive response: Discreetly pick up their clothing while feeling annoyed.

- Aggressive response: You shout at them for being dirty and disrespectful.

- Assertive response: "I am frustrated seeing your dirty clothes on the floor." I'd appreciate it if you could place them in the hamper.

- Scenario: A coworker claims credit for your effort.

- Passive response: You let things go, expecting they will ultimately recognize your effort.

- Aggressive response: accuse them of stealing your ideas.

- Assertive response: "I am surprised to hear you take credit for the project." I put in a lot of work and would want to be rewarded for it.

By practicing these scripts and role-playing various events, you may improve your assertive communication skills and gain confidence in expressing yourself.

Conflict is an unavoidable aspect of every relationship, but it does not have to be disastrous. By treating conflict constructively, you may improve your relationships and get a better knowledge of yourself and others. When confronted with conflict, take a deep breath and remind yourself that it is OK to have opposing views and viewpoints.

Avoid personal attacks and concentrate on the problem at hand. Use "I" statements to communicate your emotions and wants, and actively listen to the other person's viewpoint. Be open to compromise and find solutions that benefit both of you. If the disagreement worsens, take a break and resume the talk when you are both calmer.

Criticism may be unpleasant to hear, but it can also be an excellent chance for development. When taking criticism, strive to remain open and responsive. Listen attention to what the other person is saying and offer clarifying questions if necessary. Avoid becoming defensive or assaulting them in response.

Instead, thank them for their opinion and take some time to think about it. If the criticism is genuine, think about how you can use it to improve yourself. If it isn't valid, you may choose to disregard it and not take it personally. Remember that you are not defined by how others see you.

Mastering the skill of assertive communication allows you to convey your demands and feelings in an honest and courteous manner. You improve your relationships, settle disagreements more effectively, and develop a stronger sense of self-worth and honesty. Maya Angelou once said, "There is no greater agony than bearing an untold story inside you." By discovering your voice and expressing your truth, you break free from the shackles of silence and walk into your full potential.

Speak Your Truth with Clarity and Respect

Speaking your truth does not imply releasing a flood of emotions or screaming your grievances without filter. It is about expressing your ideas, emotions, and needs clearly and respectfully, both to yourself and to the person with whom you are interacting.

When I hesitated to express my worries throughout my relationship with Mark, my quietness, motivated by fear and a desire to avoid confrontation, further fueled the poisonous relationship. By not expressing her truth, she denied herself the chance to fight for her needs and perhaps change the relationship.

Speaking the truth involves both bravery and vulnerability. It entails venturing outside of your comfort zone and risking the judgment or rejection of others. But it's also a wonderfully freeing act, allowing you to regain your voice and advocate for what you believe in.

When telling the truth, be cautious of your tone and phrasing. Avoid using accusatory rhetoric or personal assaults. Instead, concentrate on communicating how their actions impact you. Instead of stating, "You always ignore me," add, "I'm hurt when I don't feel heard."

Be straightforward and concise in your communications. Avoid babbling and getting distracted. Express your demands and expectations clearly, without apologizing or justifying. Remember that you deserve to be heard and valued.

Speaking your truth is not about winning an argument or making a point. It's about starting a conversation, increasing understanding, and developing better connections. By talking clearly and respectfully, you create an environment for open and honest conversation in which both parties feel heard and respected.

Navigating Difficult Conversations with Grace

Even with forceful communication skills, engaging in uncomfortable discussions may seem like traversing a minefield. The emotional stakes are high, the possibility of misunderstandings exists, and the dread of confrontation may be crippling. However, by approaching these interactions with grace, you may turn them from feared ordeals to chances for personal development and connection.

During my struggle to communicate my requirements to Mark, my dread of his response kept me mute, allowing hatred to build and my spirit to fade. But what if I had approached such encounters with elegance, equipped with my newly acquired assertive communication skills? I might have expressed my concerns calmly and politely, establishing limits that prioritized my personal well-being.

Grace in tough talks requires a combination of understanding, compassion, and respect. It entails recognizing the other person's emotions while being faithful to your own. It entails approaching the topic with a desire to listen and comprehend, even if you disagree with their viewpoint.

When having unpleasant talks, it is critical to choose the correct time and venue. Avoid these interactions if you're angry, irritated, or overwhelmed. Instead, locate a quiet, secluded area where you can both concentrate on the topic without interruptions.

Begin by establishing the tone for a courteous conversation. Inform the other person that you respect their connection and wish to resolve the problem in a positive manner. Avoid accusing language or personal assaults, and instead concentrate on the precise behavior or scenario that has you concerned.

Use "I" expressions to convey your emotions and wants, and attentively listen to their responses. Recognize their viewpoint, even if you disagree with it. This does not imply giving in or compromising your own demands, but it does imply respecting their point of view.

If the talk becomes heated, take a break and resume it later when you're both calmer. It's also OK to agree to disagree. Not every argument must be resolved, and often the best approach is to just accept your differences and move on.

Unpleasant talks aren't about winning or losing. They are about establishing common ground, increasing understanding, and deepening connections. By treating these talks with kindness, you may turn them into opportunities for personal development, healing, and greater connection.

Self-Reflective Questions

1. Describe a recent interaction in which you felt unheard or misunderstood. What might you have done differently to communicate your requirements more effectively and assertively?

2. Recall a moment when you reacted quietly or forcefully to a quarrel. How might you have utilized "I" statements and active listening to help de-escalate the conflict and find a more positive solution?

3. Think about a time when you faced severe criticism. How did you react? Could you have approached it with more openness and receptivity?

4. Identify similar communication patterns in your relationships. Are they healthy and helpful, or do they lean toward passivity, violence, or passive-aggression?

5. What are your greatest worries or impediments to expressing your truth and creating boundaries? How can you overcome these difficulties and embrace aggressive communication?

Transformative Exercises

1. Challenge: For one week, use "I" expressions to describe your sentiments or wants. Consider how this change in language affects your communication and the reactions you get from others.

Transformative Exercise: Using "I" Expressions

Challenge: For one week, use "I" expressions to describe your sentiments or wants. Reflect on how this change in language affects your communication and the reactions you get from others.

Objective: The goal of this exercise is to foster more personal and accountable communication, which can lead to more meaningful and constructive interactions. By using "I" statements, you take ownership of your feelings and desires, which can help reduce defensiveness and misunderstandings in conversations.

Instructions:

1. **Identify Your Feelings and Wants:** Before speaking, take a moment to identify what you are feeling and what you need or want.
2. **Use "I" Statements:** Construct your sentences starting with "I" to express your feelings and desires clearly.

3. **Reflect Daily:** At the end of each day, take a few minutes to reflect on how using "I" expressions impacted your communication and the reactions of others.

4. **Keep a Journal:** Document your experiences, noting any changes in the way you communicate and how others respond to you.

Example Entry:

Date: Monday, June 14

Situation: During a team meeting at work, there was a disagreement about the project deadline.

Old Way of Speaking: "You never listen to my ideas, and this deadline is unreasonable."

New "I" Expression: "I feel frustrated when my ideas aren't considered, and I believe the current deadline might be too tight for us to deliver our best work."

Outcome: The team responded more positively. My colleagues acknowledged my feelings and agreed to discuss a more realistic timeline. I felt heard and valued.

Reflection: Using "I" expressions helped me communicate my feelings without sounding accusatory. It made the conversation more constructive and collaborative. Others seemed more open to listening and understanding my perspective.

Your Entry:

Date:

Situation:

Old Way of Speaking:

New "I" Expression:

Outcome:

Reflection:

Puzzle Exercise

Instruction:

Find the hidden words in the puzzle. Words can be written horizontally, vertically, or diagonally, forward or backward. Circle each word you find.

At the end of your attempt, check the Answer table to find out how correct you are.

Building Self-Love and Confidence

```
            F P N N L G J Y P N T O N L H
G B S V G D A C P U N J C I A F P F A A H J
L C S L A B R E L A T I O N S H I P S T J Q
C O M M U N I C A T I O N O W N E R S H I P
M Y Q I X U U B J Z E H F F M Y S X E X V B
X K X H O N E S T Y O O L G B V D I R H U U
E K Q M D D W X B K G E I G G W Z E T Z L E
A N D O P E N N E S S A C V Z T Y J I J N G
B Q E X P R E S S I O N T S B E Z X V O E A
V W A V Q S R F C O M P A S S I O N E Q R H
R E M P A T H Y L R E F L E C T I O N H A X
W Z I T Q A E O A L I S T E N I N G E R B T
E M N U J N P L R E B T W C P Z J G S E I N
I B O U N D A R I E S J I E T C Q R S R L C
J F R K I I O V T I W G Q C J M B A H C I U
L G V F H N X P Y E G I U K I Y Q C O U T K
L E Y B W G N B T S S U R E S P E C T Y A
H C C Z R K W X B H B S T A T E M E N T S F
```

Assertiveness	Honesty
Boundaries	Listening
Clarity	Openness
Communication	Ownership
Compassion	Reflection
Conflict	Relationships
Criticism	Respect
Empathy	Statements
Expression	Understanding
Grace	Vulnerability

Chapter 6: Healing the Wounds of the Past

The echoes of previous injuries may resonate throughout our life, producing dark shadows that block our road to healing and wholeness. Toxic relationships, in particular, may cause deep scars to fester under the surface, affecting our emotional well-being, self-esteem, and capacity to trust. However, just as the body has an inbuilt ability to repair physical damage, so does the human spirit, which enables us to heal emotional wounds.

Healing from old wounds is neither a fast cure or a band-aid solution. It's a path that demands guts, patience, and the willingness to address difficult emotions. It is about accepting the hurt, respecting the grief, and gradually letting go of the past in order to go on with newfound power and clarity.

EMDR treatment is a strong technique for trauma processing. This evidence-based therapy uses bilateral stimulation, such as eye movements or tapping, to aid in the reprocessing of traumatic memories and the reduction of emotional intensity. Individuals who access and reprocess these memories in a safe and supportive atmosphere may reduce symptoms of PTSD, anxiety, and sadness, helping them to move on from the trauma.

Cognitive Behavioral Therapy (CBT) is another excellent way to repair old wounds. This technique focuses on recognizing and overcoming negative thinking patterns and beliefs that cause emotional suffering. Individuals who learn to reframe their thinking and establish healthy coping methods may lessen anxiety, sadness, and other trauma-related symptoms.

While therapy may be an effective catalyst for healing, there are several self-guided techniques that can aid in emotional rehabilitation. Journaling, for example, may provide you a safe place to express your feelings, examine your ideas, and make sense of your experiences. Try writing out your emotions, memories, and thoughts without judgment or restriction. Allow the words to flow freely, enabling your feelings to be expressed and recognized.

Guided meditations may also help you achieve inner calm and release emotional distress. Find a peaceful area where you will not be interrupted, shut your eyes, and concentrate on your breathing. Imagine breathing in peace, love, and healing energy. As you exhale, imagine releasing tension, worry, and whatever unpleasant feelings you're holding onto.

Self-compassion is a critical part of the healing process. It entails treating oneself with care, empathy, and acceptance, particularly when you are suffering. Instead of condemning or blaming yourself for your prior experiences, provide yourself with words of encouragement and support. Remember that you are not alone in your grief, and you deserve love and compassion, particularly from yourself.

Healing from previous wounds does not mean forgetting or erasing what occurred. It is about incorporating those events into your life narrative and finding meaning and purpose in your misery. It is about turning your wounds into knowledge, and your scars into badges of bravery.

Remember that the healing process is not linear. There will be obstacles and hurdles along the road. However, with patience, effort, and the help of loved ones or specialists, you may transcend the agony of the past and build a better future. Accept the trip, since it is in the depths of our scars that we find the greatest strength and resilience.

Processing Trauma and Emotional Baggage

Consider your emotional baggage to be an old, worn-out luggage with terrible memories, regrets, and unresolved sentiments from previous poisonous relationships. This baggage, like Sarah's waning light, drags you down, preventing you from moving ahead and living a joyful and fulfilling life.

Processing trauma and emotional baggage is similar to unpacking a suitcase, carefully analyzing each item and determining what to retain, discard, and alter. It's a delicate process that takes patience, self-compassion, and the ability to face painful feelings.

Sometimes professional help is required to negotiate the complexity of trauma. Therapists trained in EMDR or CBT may provide a safe and supportive environment in which to examine your prior experiences, build coping skills, and heal old wounds. They may assist you in redefining problematic ideas, confront self-destructive routines, and create a healthy connection with yourself.

However, treatment is not the only way to recover. You may also begin on your own path of self-discovery and emotional release. Journaling helps you to pour your heart out on paper, unraveling the knots of anguish and uncertainty. Guided meditations may help you reconnect with your inner knowledge and find peace in the present moment.

Remember that healing isn't about deleting the past; it's about incorporating it into your story and finding significance in your experiences. It is about turning your anguish into purpose, and your wounds become emblems of endurance. You may emerge from the depths of pain stronger, smarter, and more powerful than you have ever been.

Find Forgiveness for Yourself and Others

Forgiveness, both for yourself and others, is an important step in healing from previous traumas. Remember Emily, who was resentful of her sacrifices throughout the years? Her road to liberty started when she finally forgiven herself for ignoring her own needs and allowed others to benefit from her goodwill.

Forgiveness does not imply tolerating the harsh conduct of others or ignoring the grief they caused. It is about releasing the hold that past behaviors have on your present and future. It is about making the decision to let go of resentment, wrath, and bitterness, not for their sake, but for your own.

Forgiving oneself is as vital. We often push ourselves to unreasonable standards, criticizing ourselves for previous errors or imagined failures. But everyone makes errors, and clinging onto self-blame simply impedes our rehabilitation.

Forgiveness is an act of self-compassion, acknowledging that we did our best with the information and resources available at the time. It's about realizing our humanity and accepting our flaws.

Forgiving people may be a difficult task, particularly when the scars are deep. But it's crucial to remember that forgiveness does not absolve them of duty. It is about releasing oneself from the weight of hatred and resentment.

Begin by admitting the harm they caused you. Allow yourself to experience grief and rage, but do not let them overtake you. Consider the conditions that may have influenced their actions. Were they also hurting? Were they acting on their own unresolved trauma?

Forgiveness does not come overnight. It's a process that requires time, patience, and the resolve to let go. It might include establishing limits, seeking treatment, or just speaking with a trusted friend or family member.

Acknowledge that forgiveness is something you offer yourself. It is not about forgetting or condemning the past, but about breaking free from its grasp. Forgiving yourself and others paves the door for healing, progress, and a peaceful and hopeful future.

Self-Reflection Questions:

1. What emotional wounds remain from prior toxic relationships?
2. Have you harbored resentment or animosity towards yourself or others for previous hurts?
3. Do you have any unfavorable thoughts or opinions based on prior experiences?

4. How can you show yourself greater love and kindness throughout your recovery journey?

5. How can you incorporate prior experiences into your life narrative and find meaning in pain?

Transformative Exercises:

1. Express forgiveness by writing a letter to yourself or someone who has wronged you. You do not have to mail it, but the act of writing might be therapeutic.

Exercise Instructions:

Expressing forgiveness can be a powerful tool for emotional healing and personal growth. This exercise involves writing a letter to yourself or someone who has wronged you. The letter can help you process your feelings and find closure. You do not have to mail it; simply writing it can be therapeutic.

1. **Find a Quiet Space**: Choose a quiet, comfortable place where you can focus without interruptions.

2. **Set Aside Time**: Allocate at least 30 minutes for this exercise to allow yourself to fully engage with your emotions.

3. **Be Honest**: Write honestly and openly about your feelings. Don't hold back – this is for your eyes only.

4. **Reflect on the Impact**: Think about how the event or situation has affected you. Consider both the negative and any potential positive outcomes.

5. **Acknowledge Your Feelings**: Allow yourself to feel and acknowledge all the emotions that come up, whether it's anger, sadness, or disappointment.

6. **Offer Forgiveness**: In your letter, explicitly state your intention to forgive. This might be to yourself for a mistake you made or to someone else for the hurt they caused you.

7. **Release and Let Go**: End your letter by expressing your intention to let go of the pain and move forward with your life.

Example Entry

Letter to Myself

Dear Me,

I know you've been carrying a lot of guilt and regret over the choices you made last year. It's been weighing heavily on you, and I can see how it's affecting your happiness and peace of mind.

You made a mistake when you decided to take on more work than you could handle, leading to burnout and neglecting your health. I understand that you were trying to prove yourself and thought you could manage everything, but it ended up taking a toll on you.

I want you to know that it's okay to make mistakes. You are human, and everyone has moments where they overestimate their limits. What's important is that you've recognized this and are taking steps to make better choices now. You are learning to prioritize your well-being and to say no when necessary.

I forgive you for pushing yourself too hard and for the consequences that came from it. Holding onto this guilt is not helping you grow. It's time to let go of the past and focus on the positive changes you're making.

From this moment on, I release you from the guilt and regret. I choose to embrace self-compassion and to move forward with a renewed sense of balance and self-care.

With love and understanding,

(Name)

Your Entry:

Puzzle Exercise

Instruction:

Find the hidden words in the puzzle. Words can be written horizontally, vertically, or diagonally, forward or backward. Circle each word you find.

At the end of your attempt, check the Answer table to find out how correct you are.

Overcoming Guilt and Self-Blame

```
            H O T E P U T Q K H V X K V L
O T S X V C P R X I Y L Z R W E X E N B N D
I X J E O Q H F S B I V K Z M V I C J S W W
V Q I T Z O C Y S A X U X K K V N R O Y J S
P Q P P R J J I O L C E I Q H M G A K P C E
G Z K B M C O M P A S S I O N P B A U K U U
M E G A T S U E H N E U J Q T L H D Y O M G
Z V F L P E R F N C D H E A L I N G C H I U
R J O D D L N E G E G H G C I X K X J R P F
L D L H E F A V F T Y H S C R Q U F T B B E
X P L O Y - L F O R G I V E N E S S H K A X
D Z A R I C I F A A A Q Y P M V L O E F G O
Y Y R T D A N X N U N M N T P D W E R K G Q
L B E D I R G A Y M I L I A H R R B A M A L
D C D E M E D I T A T I O N A L E P P S G K
G H R E S E N T M E N T D C G N T A Y O E B
L W I H O B W C D V U L N E R A B I L I T Y
S E L F - E S T E E M V L E T T I N G - G O
```

Acceptance	Pain
Baggage	Patience
Balance	Reframing
Compassion	Release
EMDR	Resentment
Forgiveness	Self-care
Healing	Self-esteem
Journaling	Therapy
Letting go	Trauma
Meditation	Vulnerability

Chapter 7: Saying "Enough" in Romantic Relationships

The whispered murmurs of unhappiness, the quiet tears shed in the seclusion of your bedroom, the nagging sensation that something isn't right—these are the obvious indicators that it's time to say "enough" in your love relationship. But how can you say this strong phrase while your heart is intertwined with another's? How can you break free from a relationship that has turned into a prison, causing agony rather than joy?

Saying "enough" in a love relationship does not have to result in a big confrontation or a tragic split. It may be a calm, forceful statement about your demands and limits. It's about respecting yourself and refusing to accept less than you deserve.

Here are some particular tactics and scripts for creating boundaries and dealing with disputes in a love relationship:

- Identify your non-negotiables. What actions are you completely reluctant to tolerate? Is it considered disrespect, dishonesty, adultery, or emotional abuse? Once you've identified your non-negotiables, you may create clear limits around them.

- Communicate your needs: Don't assume your spouse understands your requirements or how their conduct impacts you. Be straightforward and explicit in your message. Express your sentiments and requirements using "I" phrases, rather than blaming or criticizing others. For instance, rather of stating, "You never listen to me," assert, "I feel unheard when I'm talking to you, and I would appreciate it if you could put your phone down and give me your full attention."

- Be ready for pushback: Your spouse may be upset when you start establishing limits, particularly if they are used to getting their way. Maintain your composure and conviction. Remember that you are not responsible for how others respond to your limits.

- Enforce penalties. If your spouse consistently breaks your limits, be prepared to enforce the penalties. This might include taking a vacation from the relationship, seeking couples' treatment, or quitting the partnership if they refuse to change.

- Prioritize your well-being: Your needs and emotions are legitimate. You should be treated with love, respect, and concern. Don't compromise your health for the sake of the connection.

Saying "enough" is not indicative of weakness or failure. It's a demonstration of bravery, self-love, and empowerment. It's about recognizing your value and refusing to accept less than you deserve. It's about taking control of your life and creating a future that is consistent with your beliefs and goals.

Recognizing Red Flags and Deal Breakers

In the exhilarating cloud of new love, it's easy to miss the subtle warning signals that a relationship isn't as healthy as it seems. Toxic relationships, like a vividly colored deadly frog, can hide their actual nature under beauty and attraction. However, beyond the surface, there are often red flags and dealbreakers that, if ignored, may lead to misery and disappointment.

Red flags may appear in a variety of forms, ranging from subtle insults and passive-aggressive remarks to open verbal abuse and physical assault. They might include domineering conduct, envy, dishonesty, manipulation, or a lack of empathy.

Dealbreakers, on the other hand, are non-negotiable principles or behaviors that you cannot tolerate in a relationship. These might include adultery, addiction, a history of violence, or a fundamental difference in beliefs and life objectives.

Recognizing red flags and dealbreakers is critical for avoiding a toxic relationship. It's about recognizing your value and refusing to accept less than you deserve.

Here are some frequent red flags and deal breakers to look out for:

- Controlling behavior: Does your spouse attempt to influence your behaviors, choices, or relationships? Do they alienate you from your loved ones or make you feel bad about spending time with others?
- Jealousy and insecurity: Is your spouse accusing you of flirting or cheating? Do they track your phone or social media? Do they make you feel as if you cannot be trusted?
- Does your spouse show disrespect by belittling you, criticizing your looks, or dismissing your feelings? Do they speak down to you, making you feel tiny and insignificant?
- Dishonesty and manipulation: Does your spouse lie, conceal facts, or twist words? Do they make you feel guilty or accountable for their emotions?

- Lack of empathy: Does your spouse disregard your emotions or needs? Do they reject your worries or make you believe you're overreacting?

If you observe any of these red flags in your relationship, address them right away. Discuss your worries with your spouse, create clear limits, and seek professional treatment if required. Remember that you deserve to be in a healthy, loving relationship that promotes your development and well-being. Do not settle for anything less.

Walking Away from Love Addiction

Sometimes the most difficult "enough" we can say is to a love that has become an addiction, a poisonous habit masquerading as enthusiasm.

Love addiction, like any other addiction, is characterized by a compulsive need for a "fix," or a frantic need for the emotional high provided by the object of our love. We stick to the relationship, even when it is plainly toxic, because we are afraid of the loneliness and agony that comes with being alone.

We are pulled back to our relationship like a moth to a flame, even if we know they would burn us. In a frantic desire to keep the relationship alive, we disregard warning signs, excuse their harmful conduct, and compromise our own needs. However, this constant quest of love only causes more suffering and disappointment.

Breaking away from love addiction requires identifying the toxic patterns that enslave us. It entails admitting that the relationship is not founded on true love, but rather on toxic dependence. It entails acknowledging that we deserve a relationship that feeds and uplifts us, rather than one that leaves us feeling empty and shattered.

Breaking out from love addiction is a brave act of self-love. It's about prioritizing your own well-being above the brief highs and crushing lows of a poisonous relationship. It is about ending the pattern of reliance and recovering your ability to live a life full of healthy, happy love.

This path might include seeking professional treatment, joining a support group, or just confiding in trustworthy friends and family. It is important to surround oneself with individuals who understand what you are going through and can provide advice and support.

Many individuals have conquered their love addictions and gone on to enjoy healthy, satisfying relationships. Saying "enough" to the addicted love opens the door to a really free love.

Self-Reflection Questions:

1. Identify non-negotiables in your love relationship. Which actions or beliefs are extremely necessary for you to feel secure, respected, and loved?

2. Have you identified any red flags or dealbreakers in your present or previous relationships? How did you reply to them? Did you ignore, rationalize, or confront them front on?

3. Do you have indications of love addiction, such as a compulsive desire for attention, fear of desertion, or prioritizing your partner's demands above your own?

4. How can you express your wants and limits more effectively in romantic relationships? Are there any communication practices you should change?

5. How do you see a good, successful love relationship? What attributes are you looking for in a companion, and how do you want to be treated?

Transformative Exercises:

1. Create a Self-Care Plan: Establish a daily habit that supports your mind, body, and soul. This might include activities such as exercise, meditation, writing, spending time in nature, or pursuing hobbies and interests that you like.

Create a Self-Care Plan: Transformative Exercise

Establishing a self-care plan is essential for maintaining balance and well-being. This exercise will guide you in creating a daily habit that supports your mind, body, and soul. Follow the steps below and refer to the example entry to help you get started.

Steps to Create Your Self-Care Plan:

1. **Identify Your Needs**: Reflect on what activities make you feel rejuvenated and fulfilled. Consider different aspects of your well-being: physical, emotional, and spiritual.

2. **Set Realistic Goals**: Choose activities that you can incorporate into your daily routine without feeling overwhelmed. Start small and build gradually.

3. **Schedule Your Activities**: Dedicate specific times in your day for self-care activities. Consistency is key to establishing a habit.

4. **Track Your Progress**: Keep a journal or use an app to monitor your activities and how they make you feel. Adjust your plan as needed.

Example Self-Care Plan Entry

Name:

Date: June 14, 2024

Mind

- **Activity**: Morning Meditation

- **Time**: 7:00 AM - 7:15 AM

- **Description**: Spend 15 minutes in guided meditation to start the day with a calm and focused mind.

- **Benefits**: Reduces stress, improves concentration, and enhances emotional well-being.

Body

- **Activity**: Yoga Session

- **Time**: 6:00 PM - 6:30 PM

- **Description**: Practice a 30-minute yoga routine focusing on stretching and relaxation.

- **Benefits**: Increases flexibility, strengthens muscles, and promotes relaxation.

Soul

- **Activity**: Nature Walk

- **Time**: 8:00 AM - 8:30 AM

- **Description**: Take a 30-minute walk in the nearby park to connect with nature and enjoy fresh air.

- **Benefits**: Boosts mood, reduces anxiety, and fosters a sense of peace and connection.

Reflection

- **Journal Entry**: At the end of each day, spend 10 minutes writing about your experiences with the self-care activities. Note any changes in your mood, energy levels, and overall well-being.

Your Entry:

Name:

Date:

Mind

- **Activity**:

- **Time**:

- **Description**:

- **Benefits**:

Body

- **Activity**:

- **Time**:

- **Description**:

- **Benefits**:

Soul

- **Activity**:

- **Time**:

- **Description**:

- **Benefits**:

Reflection

Puzzle Exercise

Instruction:

Find the hidden words in the puzzle. Words can be written horizontally, vertically, or diagonally, forward or backward. Circle each word you find.

At the end of your attempt, check the Answer table to find out how correct you are.

Developing Emotional Resilience

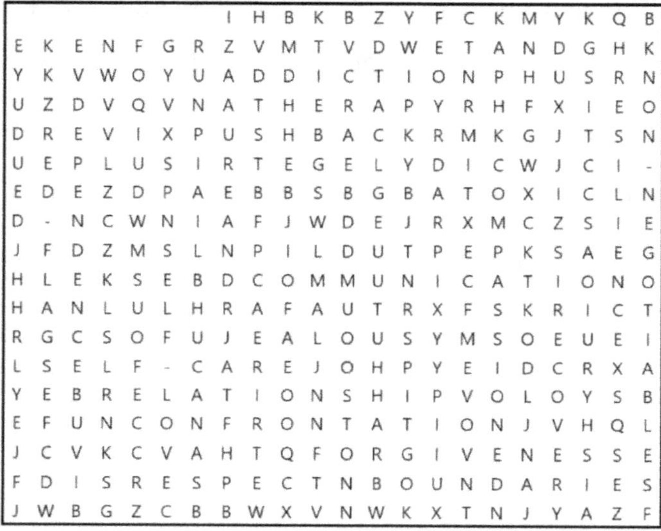

Addiction

Boundaries

Communication

Compassion

Confrontation

Dealbreakers

Dependence

Disrespect

Forgiveness

Jealousy

Non-negotiables

Pushback

Recovery

Red flags

Relationship

Resilience

Self-care

Self-love

Therapy

Toxic

Chapter 8: Saying "Enough" in Family Relationships

Family links, formed through shared history and unconditional love, may be the most reassuring and supporting in our lives. However, these same relationships may become twisted and confining, providing a breeding ground for pain, hatred, and dysfunction. Saying "enough" amid the complex web of family relationships may seem like an impossible task, laden with shame, anxiety, and the weight of unsaid expectations. But, just as a sapling need space to develop, so does the human soul, even within the boundaries of family affection.

Saying "enough" in family connections should not imply cutting links or leaving loved ones. It is about establishing healthy boundaries, articulating your requirements clearly, and refusing to accept conduct that is harmful to your well-being. It's about recognizing yourself and establishing an environment in which you can flourish, even in the midst of familial dynamics.

Here are some particular tactics and scripts for establishing boundaries and dealing with disagreements in family relationships:

- Identify your triggers. What habits or events in your family cause unpleasant feelings or reactions? Once you've identified your triggers, you may begin to put limits around them.
- If you're new to creating limits, start with tiny measures. For example, instead of attending every family function, gently refuse invites to gatherings that sap your energy or elicit unpleasant feelings.
- Use "I" phrases to convey emotions and needs without criticizing or blaming others. Instead of stating, "You always criticize me," respond, "I am hurt when you criticize my decisions." I'd like it if you could show more support."
- Enforce repercussions for family members who persistently break your limits. This might include restricting contact, eliminating harmful talks, or even taking a short vacation from the relationship if required.
- Seek assistance: Talking to a therapist or joining a support group may help you manage difficult family relationships.

Remember that declaring "enough" in family connections does not imply rejecting or excluding people from your life. It is about developing healthy dynamics, establishing boundaries that respect your well-being, and cultivating more real and rewarding relationships. It is about choosing to love your family while simultaneously loving yourself.

Navigating Complex Family Dynamics

Family relations, like the complex roots of an old tree, may become entangled, entwined, and deeply entrenched. The hidden norms, generational habits, and implicit expectations all add to a tangled web that may be hard to untangle.

Managing complicated family interactions requires a precise mix of empathy, assertiveness, and self-awareness. It is about identifying the patterns that have structured your family's relationships and comprehending how they have affected you. It's about recognizing the responsibilities you've been given and evaluating if they genuinely benefit your well-being.

It's crucial to realize that you're not in charge of correcting or modifying your family's conduct. You only have control over your own actions and emotions. Setting healthy boundaries, articulating your needs clearly, and refusing to accept harmful conduct can allow you to survive within the family system.

This might include having uncomfortable talks, confronting long-held views, or even separating yourself from family members who refuse to respect your limits. It's not an easy journey, but it's essential for individuals who want to recover their power and live truthfully.

Remember, you are not alone on this path. Many individuals suffer with complicated family relationships. Seek help from therapists, support groups, or trustworthy friends who can provide advice and understanding. By negotiating these intricacies with bravery and compassion, you may build a stronger, more satisfying connection with your family, one that respects your needs while allowing you to shine your own unique light.

Setting Boundaries Between Parents and Siblings

Within the close domain of family, the borders between affection, obligation, and personal liberty may blur, making it particularly difficult to set and maintain appropriate boundaries. For many people, declaring "enough" to parents or siblings may elicit deep-seated anxieties of rejection, shame, or even the breakdown of family connections. However, as Anya's tale shows, creating boundaries with loved ones is not an act of rebellion, but rather a necessary step toward self-preservation and healthy relationships.

When interacting with parents, keep in mind that they, too, are on a path of personal development and discovery. They might have their own unresolved traumas, persistent routines, or just differing viewpoints on life. While we cannot change their conduct, we can alter how we respond to it.

If your parents constantly criticize your choices or provide unsolicited advice, gently remind them that you are an adult who can make your own decisions. You might respond, "I appreciate your concern, but I am secure in my decisions. "Please respect my autonomy."

If your parents are excessively engaged in your life, establish clear limits for communication and personal space. Tell them that you appreciate their love and support, but you also need space to live your own life. You may say, "I love you and enjoy spending time with you, but I also need time for me. Please respect my request for privacy.

Setting boundaries with siblings may be as difficult, particularly if you grew up in a competitive or emotionally charged atmosphere. If your siblings continuously disparage you or attempt to dominate your life, you must stand up for yourself and set clear boundaries.

You might say, "I love you, but I will not accept being talked to in that manner. Please show greater consideration for my sentiments." Or, "I appreciate your advice, but I can make my own decisions." Please trust my judgement."

Setting limits with family members does not imply that you love them any less. It simply implies that you value yourself enough to prioritize your own well-being. It's about establishing an environment in which you can be your true self, free of the restraints of toxic family relations.

Creating limits is a continual effort. It takes perseverance, persistence, and a willingness to express your requirements clearly and assertively. However, the benefits are worthwhile. Establishing appropriate boundaries with your family allows you to build more real and rewarding connections while also respecting your own path of self-discovery and personal progress.

Self-Reflection Questions:

1. How have family dynamics influenced your perceptions about yourself and your position in relationships?
2. Are there any unwritten norms or expectations in your family that you may be unintentionally honoring, even if they are no longer relevant to you?
3. What actions or events in your family cause emotions of guilt, anger, or anxiety?
4. Establishing limits with parents or siblings may promote well-being and healthy relationships.

5. What are your thoughts or anxiety about expressing "enough" to family? What strategies can you take to overcome these fears?

Transformative Exercises:

1. Develop a regular self-compassion practice by speaking nicely to yourself, forgiving past faults, and recognizing your intrinsic value. This practice may help you develop resilience and inner strength, making it easier to establish and keep appropriate limits.

Transformative Exercise for Developing Self-Compassion

Step 1: Speak Nicely to Yourself

Goal: Replace negative self-talk with positive affirmations.

Exercise:

- Each morning, stand in front of the mirror and say three positive things about yourself. These can be related to your character, abilities, or accomplishments.
- Write down these affirmations in a journal.

Example Entry:

- "I am capable and strong."

- "I have a kind heart and always try to help others."

- "I am proud of my progress and the effort I put into my health."

Step 2: Forgive Past Faults

Goal: Release yourself from the burden of past mistakes.

Exercise:

- Reflect on a past mistake or regret. Write it down in your journal, acknowledging what happened without judgment.
- Write a letter of forgiveness to yourself, expressing understanding and compassion for your past self.

Example Entry:

Mistake: "I regret not sticking to my exercise routine last year."

Forgiveness Letter:

- "Dear Sophie, I forgive you for not maintaining your exercise routine. You were going through a challenging time, and it's okay to have setbacks. What matters is that you are trying again and learning from the past. I am proud of your commitment to improve."

Step 3: Recognize Your Intrinsic Value

Goal: Understand and appreciate your inherent worth, independent of external achievements.

Exercise:

- Spend a few minutes each day reflecting on your inherent qualities that make you valuable. These should not be tied to accomplishments but rather to who you are as a person.
- Write these reflections in your journal.

Example Entry:

- "I am valuable because I am compassionate and always willing to listen to others."

- "My worth comes from my ability to love and be loved, just as I am."

- "I have intrinsic value because I strive to be a better person every day."

Step 4: Develop Resilience and Inner Strength

Goal: Build resilience by consistently practicing self-compassion.

Exercise:

- Each week, review your journal entries. Notice patterns and progress. Reflect on how speaking nicely to yourself, forgiving your faults, and recognizing your value have impacted your resilience.

- Set small goals to reinforce your practice of self-compassion, such as meditating for five minutes a day or practicing gratitude.

Example Entry:

Weekly Reflection:

- "This week, I noticed that I felt less stressed and more confident. Speaking kindly to myself helped me face challenges without self-doubt. Forgiving my past mistakes has allowed me to focus on the present. Recognizing my intrinsic value made me feel worthy and capable of setting healthy boundaries."

Goal for Next Week:

- "Continue with morning affirmations and add a five-minute meditation focusing on self-love. Practice gratitude by writing down three things I'm thankful for each evening."

Your Entry:

Speak Nicely to Yourself

Forgive Past Faults

Recognize Your Intrinsic Value

Develop Resilience and Inner Strength

Puzzle Exercise

Instruction:

Find the hidden words in the puzzle. Words can be written horizontally, vertically, or diagonally, forward or backward. Circle each word you find.

At the end of your attempt, check the Answer table to find out how correct you are.

The Process of Forgiveness

```
            H V S V Y Y O L K F E C F D K
Z H B L W H G P R B F M B O U N D A R I E S
N N T R I G G E R S C C O M P A S S I O N D
W N V A K M F H C U L V T R E J E C T I O N
H E L R Z W I Q R P X T A J O T L B I P C E
W G L E Q U N T I P G U I L T F F C C L K
M O I L O E U Z S O V H N N L A - O I O H P
W T H A - S B J H R S M V E O M C N S M J T
L I H T A B L A U T O N O M Y I O F M M R
I A L I V A E M N B N D L U F L M R C U A H
T T A O G X E I O P R I V A C Y P O K N F P
Z E G N X Z U S N U N D E R S T A N D I N G
M Y K S V W C W T G V U M F Z V S T E C Y H
C O B H A K B D H X H C E V W U S A P A O G
U Q V I N D E P E N D E N C E U I T G T D F
X G L P D Y O O B R R D T I X U O I H I K V
D X O S Z A X A E R T B N C M V N O K O W D
E Q Z I I S B E E Q G Q M M F A R N J N P F
```

Autonomy	Limits
Boundaries	Negotiate
Communication	Privacy
Compassion	Rejection
Confrontation	Relationships
Criticism	Self-compassion
Family	Support
Guilt	Triggers
Independence	Understanding
Involvement	Well-being

Chapter 9: Saying "Enough" in the Workplace

The office, which is typically praised as a professional paradise, may sometimes devolve into a battlefield of subtle hostility, power battles, and emotional manipulation. The insidious nature of workplace toxicity may leave you feeling exhausted, underappreciated, and doubting your own worth. However, just as a good diplomat navigates complicated foreign relations, you can also learn to set appropriate limits and state your demands at work.

Let's go over some practical methods and scripts for stating "enough" in the workplace:

1.   Identify your non-negotiables.

What are some things you would not accept in the workplace? Is it disrespect, unrealistic expectations, or a lack of recognition? Once you've identified your non-negotiables, you may create clear limits around them. For example, if you value work-life balance, you may set a rule that you would not answer business emails or calls after a specific time.

2. Communicate clearly and directly.

Avoid ambiguity and sugarcoating in your message. Be straightforward and explicit in expressing your requirements and concerns. Use "I" expressions to communicate your emotions without blaming or accusing. For example, instead of stating, "You often dump work on me at the last minute," say, "I become overwhelmed when I get last-minute projects. I'd appreciate it if you could give me more notice in the future.

3. Document everything.

Keep track of any discussions, emails, and occasions when your boundaries have been broken. This paperwork might be very useful if you need to escalate the situation to HR or a higher authority.

4. Seek Support:

Speak with a trustworthy coworker, mentor, or HR representative. They can provide advice and assistance as you negotiate difficult employment circumstances.

5. Know Your Rights:

Understand your company's rules and processes for workplace harassment, discrimination, and retribution. This information will provide you the ability to take action if your boundaries are breached.

6. Prepare to walk away:

If your company repeatedly ignores your limits and creates a hostile work atmosphere, don't be scared to go elsewhere. Your health is more crucial than any work.

Here are some more scripts for creating limits in the workplace.

- Tell a coworker who repeatedly interrupts you, "I appreciate your enthusiasm, but I'm trying to focus on this task." Could we please discuss this later?
- For a manager that micromanages: "I understand you want to be kept in the loop, but I'm confident in my ability to handle this project." I'll keep you posted on my progress, but I'd prefer it if you trusted me to perform my job."
- To a colleague who gossips: "I don't like discussing other people's personal lives." Could you kindly alter the subject?

Remember, stating "enough" in the job does not imply being unpleasant or aggressive. It's about standing up for yourself, maintaining your health, and establishing a work atmosphere in which you can flourish. Setting healthy limits and properly stating your demands can allow you to recover your power and live a more rewarding and empowered work life.

Dealing With Toxic Coworkers and Bosses

Toxic coworkers and managers may foster a culture of dread, anxiety, and poor morale. Their actions might vary from subtle undermining to open bullying, leaving you exhausted, demotivated, and doubting your own talents.

But remember, you have the authority to declare, "Enough." It is not about participating in a power struggle or lowering yourself to their level. It's about creating clear boundaries, preserving your well-being, and refusing to be a victim of their poisonous behavior.

When dealing with a toxic coworker, try to restrict your encounters with them as much as possible. Maintain a professional demeanor during your interactions and avoid becoming involved in their drama. If they attempt to drag you into gossip or negativity, simply excuse yourself or change the topic.

If a colleague's conduct has a direct impact on your job, don't be afraid to confront the matter immediately. Use "I" sentences to explain how their conduct affects you and provide a remedy. For example, if a coworker often interrupts you during meetings, you may explain, "I feel as if my contributions are not being heard when I am interrupted. Could we perhaps wait for each other to complete our ideas before leaping in?

Dealing with a toxic employer might be more difficult because of the power imbalance that often exists. However, it is still necessary to advocate for yourself and establish clear limits. If your employer is regularly overwhelming you with work, say something like, "I'm committed to doing my best work, but I'm feeling overwhelmed by my current workload." Could we talk about prioritizing my duties and creating more realistic deadlines?

If your supervisor is verbally abusive or creates a hostile work environment, you should record the instances and seek help from HR or a trustworthy coworker. Remember that you have the right to work in a safe, respected atmosphere.

Dealing with toxic coworkers and employers might be exhausting, but remember that you're not alone. Many individuals have overcome comparable circumstances and emerged stronger on the other side. Setting limits, talking assertively, and getting help when required may help you safeguard your well-being while also creating a more pleasant and powerful work environment.

Advocating For Your Needs and Rights

When we allow ourselves to be stomped on, overworked, or underpaid, we not only jeopardize our own well-being, but also contribute to a culture of contempt and exploitation.

Advocating for your wants and rights in the workplace does not imply being selfish or demanding. It is about acknowledging your intrinsic worth as an employee and a human being. It's about sticking up for what you deserve and refusing to accept less.

This includes speaking out if you're feeling overwhelmed or unappreciated. It entails requesting the assistance and resources required to do your duties efficiently. It implies refusing to be treated with contempt or condescension.

Advocacy may take several forms. It might include speaking directly with your manager about your workload or asking further training to improve your abilities. It might include speaking up in a meeting to express your thoughts or concerns. Or it might simply mean saying "no" to things that are outside of your job description or those you are unable to do.

Remember that your voice matters. Your requirements are important. Your rights are important. Never be scared to stand out and advocate for yourself. By doing so, you not only enhance your personal work experience but also help to create a more pleasant and powerful workplace culture for everyone.

Self-Reflective Questions:

1. What are your non-negotiables at work? Consider the values and limits that are most important to you. What are the things you just will not tolerate?

2. Have you ever felt underappreciated or abused at work? How did you handle such situations? Do you wish you had handled things differently?

3. What are your top anxieties or obstacles while advocating for oneself at work? Are you terrified of confrontation, rejection, or unpleasant outcomes?

4. How can you convey your requirements more effectively and assertively? Consider using "I" statements, recording interactions, and getting help from trustworthy coworkers or mentors.

5. What are your long-term professional goals? How can establishing limits and advocating for yourself help you accomplish your goals?

Transformative Exercise:

1. Prepare a "Workplace Boundaries" worksheet. Divide a piece of paper into three columns: "Non-negotiables," "Boundaries," and "Consequences." Fill out each section with concrete examples from your company.

Workplace Boundaries Worksheet

Instructions:

1. **Non-negotiables**: These are the essential principles or conditions you must have to function effectively and maintain your well-being at work.
2. **Boundaries**: These are specific limits you set to protect your non-negotiables and maintain a healthy work environment.
3. **Consequences**: These are the actions you will take if your boundaries are not respected.

Example Entry:

Non-negotiables	Boundaries	Consequences
Work-Life Balance	No work emails or calls after 7 PM	Politely decline to respond to non-urgent emails/calls until the next workday.
Respectful Communication	No yelling or derogatory language in meetings	Address the issue directly with the person involved; escalate to HR if necessary.

Designated Break Times	Take a full hour for lunch break without interruptions	Decline meetings or calls scheduled during break times; communicate availability clearly.
Personal Workspace Privacy	Knock before entering someone's office or cubicle	Address intrusions with a reminder about personal space; escalate repeated offenses to a supervisor.
Professional Development Opportunities	Attend at least one training session per quarter	Prioritize scheduling and request time off for professional development; address conflicts with management.
Clear Role Responsibilities	Job duties should align with job description	Discuss and clarify role expectations with supervisor; document and

		address ongoing discrepancies.
	117	

Your Entry:

Puzzle Exercise

Instruction:

Find the hidden words in the puzzle. Words can be written horizontally, vertically, or diagonally, forward or backward. Circle each word you find.

At the end of your attempt, check the Answer table to find out how correct you are.

Developing Healthy Connections

```
            U N A P P R E C I A T E D K M
Y K F M V Z W I V J D L S R N V Z O O Y M J
E W N Z M W N T U L P P W W N K Z V V R X S
D A N C M T M T X K F W O R K P L A C E V E
V L Z O O I G J Z W M A U C P R R V O S C L
U T Q N D O C U M E N T A T I O N H V P P F
T R U S T W O R T H Y O T H D F O F E E D -
I A T E N A D V O C A C Y T O E Y D R C T A
O N Z Q P D P H Q M E K D I V S D B W T O D
L S W U X J Y G D P A H C I L S T R H J X V
C P A E F I T B R N Q N B S N I N I E A I O
C A F N K K H L D S M W A D U O S G L A C C
Z R S C N V E X O D E U O G T N M H M I I A
O E U E M P O W E R M E N T E A U T E F T C
V N L S U P P O R T G A J W R L A S D Z Y Y
F C J O J F N O N - N E G O T I A B L E S Z
J Y Q N X O W J P M Y H A R A S S M E N T A
Q V B O U N D A R I E S O Z P M X R R H J L
```

Advocacy	Professionalism
Boundaries	Respect
Consequences	Rights
Documentation	Self-advocacy
Empowerment	Support
Harassment	Toxicity
Hostility	Transparency
Micromanage	Trustworthy
Non-negotiables	Unappreciated
Overwhelmed	Workplace

Chapter 10: Saying "Enough" to Self-Sabotage

Self-sabotage lurks as a powerful foe, a smart saboteur who destroys our development and keeps us linked to recurrent patterns of sorrow and failure. It's the voice that whispers doubts in our ears, the hand that trips us just as we're about to cross the finish line, and the unseen force that sabotages our hopes and goals.

Perhaps you've been frustrated by undermining your own success, whether it's delaying on a critical assignment, engaging in bad behaviors despite your best intentions, or self-destructing promising relationships. The causes for self-sabotage are often complicated and deeply founded in our subconscious beliefs and experiences.

At its foundation, self-sabotage is a defensive strategy used to shield oneself from the perceived danger of failure, rejection, or change. It's a perverse type of self-preservation motivated by a fear of the unknown and the conviction that we don't deserve pleasure or success.

For others, self-sabotage arises from a lack of self-esteem. We may feel that we aren't good enough, clever enough, or capable of accomplishing our objectives. We could feel unworthy of love, prosperity, or pleasure. These negative ideas become self-fulfilling prophesies, causing us to unintentionally destroy ourselves in order to validate our darkest fears.

Others may self-sabotage out of a fear of achievement. The thought of realizing our aspirations may be both thrilling and scary. We may be concerned that success would alter us, alienate us, or leave us exposed to criticism and judgment. To avoid these imagined hazards, we may unintentionally hinder our own efforts, ensuring that we never attain the heights we dread.

Childhood events may also play an important part in self-sabotage. If we grew up in an environment that ignored our needs or rejected our successes, we may develop a feeling of unworthiness or the conviction that we do not deserve wonderful things. These deeply established ideas may materialize as self-defeating actions in adulthood, creating a cycle of self-doubt and self-destruction.

Recognizing and halting negative thinking patterns is an important step towards resolving self-sabotage. Our ideas have enormous influence on our emotions and behaviors. When we let negative ideas take over our thinking, we create a self-fulfilling prophesy of failure and disappointment.

Begin by being aware of your inner critic, that nagging voice that continuously assesses, criticizes, and mocks you. Pay attention to how you define yourself and your experiences. Are they pleasant and encouraging, or harsh and self-deprecating?

When you see yourself participating in negative self-talk, counter your ideas with positive affirmations. Instead of stating "I'm not good enough," say, "I am worthy and capable of achieving my goals." Instead of stating, "I'll never be able to do this," try saying, "I am willing to learn and grow, and I am open to new possibilities."

Positive self-talk does not include rejecting reality or assuming that everything is fine. It's about choosing to concentrate on your strengths, acknowledging your achievements, and building a more positive and empowered mentality.

In addition to affirmations, there are other tools and approaches for disrupting negative thinking patterns. Mindfulness activities like meditation and deep breathing may help you become more aware of your thoughts and emotions, enabling you to react to them more effectively.

Gratitude activities, such as maintaining a gratitude diary or writing thank-you cards, may help you shift your attention away from what is wrong in your life and toward what is good. Developing a grateful mindset may help you reprogram your brain for optimism and abundance.

Seeking help from a therapist or counselor may be quite beneficial in overcoming self-sabotage. A therapist may assist you in identifying the underlying reasons of your self-destructive habits, developing healthy coping skills, and devising a long-term transformation strategy.

Overcoming self-sabotage is a process, not a destination. Confronting your innermost fears and anxieties requires time, work, and willingness. However, by increasing self-awareness, confronting negative thinking patterns, and adopting positive self-talk, you may regain your power and live a life that reflects your actual potential.

Breaking Free of Negative Thought Patterns

Negative thought patterns are the subtle whispers of self-doubt that reverberate in our brains, casting shadows on our self-esteem and potential. They keep repeating the same stale tunes: "I'm not good enough," "I'll never succeed," or "I don't deserve happiness." These ideas, which are often based on prior experiences and deeply held beliefs, may become self-fulfilling prophesies, causing us to subconsciously destroy our own pleasure and success.

Breaking away from these negative thinking patterns is like untangling a knot; it's a delicate process that demands time, self-compassion, and the courage to question our strongly held ideas. It is about acknowledging that our opinions are not facts, but rather interpretations of reality influenced by our own prejudices and experiences.

The first stage is to become conscious of the negative thinking patterns. Pay attention to the tales you tell yourself about yourself and your experiences. Are they powerful and inspiring, or are they restricting and self-deprecating? Do you obsess about previous errors or worry about potential failures?

After you've discovered your negative thinking patterns, confront them with facts to the contrary. Find a positive counter-thought to every negative one. For example, if you find yourself thinking, "I'm not good enough," remind yourself of your previous accomplishments and the positive attributes that distinguish you.

Replace self-criticism with compassion. Treat yourself with the same love and understanding that you would provide to a friend. Remember that everyone makes errors, and your value is not determined by your defects or inadequacies.

Mindfulness helps you become more aware of your thoughts and emotions. When negative thoughts come, examine them without judgment and gently bring your focus back to the present moment. This may be as easy as concentrating on your breath, recognizing your body's feelings, or indulging in a relaxing activity such as walking or listening to music.

By continuously questioning negative thinking patterns and replacing them with positive affirmations, you may rewire your brain for optimism and self-belief. This process takes time and work, but with practice, you can overcome self-sabotage and develop a more empowered story for your life.

Cultivating Self-Compassion and Acceptance

Self-compassion is the antidote to self-destructive behavior. It's the warm hug we give ourselves when we fail, the calm voice whispering, "You are worthy, you are loved, and you are enough." It is the awareness that we are all human, flawed, and prone to error.

Imagine self-compassion as a loving parent who loves and supports us unconditionally, even when we make mistakes. It is the polar opposite of the harsh inner critic, who berates us for our flaws and exacerbates our fears.

Cultivating self-compassion entails learning to be nice to ourselves, to forgive ourselves for our errors, and to accept our flaws. It is about acknowledging that we are deserving of love and respect, regardless of our successes or failings.

Self-kindness is one technique that might help you develop self-compassion. This entails treating oneself with the same compassion and understanding that you would provide to a friend in distress. When you make a mistake, instead of punishing yourself, give yourself words of encouragement and support. Remind yourself that everyone makes errors and that this is just a learning experience.

Recognizing our shared humanity is a crucial part of self-compassion. This entails admitting that we are all flawed, that we struggle, and that we make errors. Recognizing that we are not alone in our challenges might make us feel less alone and humiliated.

Finally, self-compassion entails practicing mindfulness, or paying attention to the present moment without judgment. When we are attentive, we can examine our thoughts and feelings without being caught up in them. This enables us to address our difficulties with more clarity and compassion.

By practicing self-compassion and acceptance, we create a secure and caring environment inside ourselves in which we may heal, grow, and flourish. We break away from the cycle of self-sabotage and allow ourselves to imagine a life full of love, pleasure, and satisfaction.

Self-Reflection Questions:

1. Identify frequent negative thinking patterns in yourself. Take a minute to notice the common statements or attitudes that often impair your confidence and potential.

2. In which areas of my life do I self-sabotage? Is it related to your relationships, job, health, or personal goals? Identifying particular issues might help you solve them more effectively.

3. Identify any underlying concerns or anxieties that may be motivating self-sabotage behaviors. Do you fear failure, rejection, success, or the unknown? Understanding the fundamental reasons allows you to address them at their source.

4. How do I communicate to myself after making a mistake or experiencing a setback? Is your internal conversation friendly and encouraging, or harsh and critical? Examining your self-talk might reflect how much you really appreciate yourself.

5. What favorable attributes and abilities do I typically ignore or downplay? Recognizing your own value and potential is critical for overcoming self-sabotage.

Transformative Exercises:

1. Create a thankfulness journal: Every day, list three things you're thankful for. This simple technique might help you change your emphasis from negativity to optimism and develop a more cheerful mindset.

Transformative Exercise: Create a Thankfulness Journal

Practicing gratitude can significantly improve your overall well-being by shifting your focus from negativity to positivity. By regularly acknowledging the things you're thankful for, you can cultivate a more cheerful and optimistic mindset. Follow the steps below to start your thankfulness journal.

Steps to Create Your Thankfulness Journal:

1. **Choose a Journal**: Select a dedicated notebook or use a digital journal app where you can write down your thoughts daily.

2. **Set a Routine**: Decide on a specific time each day to make your entries. Morning or evening works well, as it sets a positive tone for the day or helps you reflect on the day's events.

3. **Write Three Things**: Every day, list three things you're thankful for. They can be big or small, simple or significant. The key is consistency and genuine reflection.

Example Entry:

Date: June 13, 2024

1. **Sunrise Walk**: This morning's walk during sunrise was incredibly peaceful. The fresh air and beautiful colors of the sky filled me with a sense of calm and gratitude.

2. **Supportive Friend**: I'm thankful for my friend, Emily, who called to check on me today. Her kindness and support always lift my spirits.

3. **Healthy Meal**: I enjoyed a delicious and nourishing dinner made from fresh, whole foods. It reminded me of the importance of taking care of my body and making healthy choices.

Your Entry:

Date: June 13, 2024

1. **Sunrise Walk**:

2. **Supportive Friend**:

3. **Healthy Meal**:

Puzzle Exercise

Instruction:

Find the hidden words in the puzzle. Words can be written horizontally, vertically, or diagonally, forward or backward. Circle each word you find.

At the end of your attempt, check the Answer table to find out how correct you are.

Healing and Nurturing Your Inner Child

```
        S E L F - D E S T R U C T I V E
G   A U U J S O F D R H D Q P M N J S G P D
N R E F L E C T I O N Y P R K B D C A S R R
G C A J X A I V F D T S E L F - E S T E E M
D O O T C A C C E P T A N C E V Y E M E S D
W N L V I Z T H S E L F - S A B O T A G E B
A F Y L C T J H I O L F L Z A T S H Q I R G
Y I D P C O U N T E R - T H O U G H T M V K
D D Q N Y O W D Z G V P X P O T E N T I A L
S E N H X V J K E N C E T L A O C X J N T Y
E N S M W E F D O E A P M M P T V U P D I L
L C O F P R O G M G M V X E G F T M N F O P
S E L F - C O M P A S S I O N M M E T U N R
J F K D A O M I S T X V H O P T N I R L A Z
W H V S R M G R Y I C O M P A S S I O N Z X
C N A A D I C C G V F A L A W A R E N E S S
F D F O P N Q N J E R W O R T H I N E S S S
D N P P E G Y Z A F F I R M A T I O N S R Y
```

Acceptance	Overcoming
Achievements	Patterns
Affirmations	Potential
Awareness	Preservation
Compassion	Reflection
Confidence	Self-compassion
Counter-thought	Self-destructive
Gratitude	Self-esteem
Mindfulness	Self-sabotage
Negative	Worthiness

Chapter 11: Embracing Your Authentic Self

Emerging from the shadows of toxic relationships, a bright reality awaits: the embrace of your true self. This chapter is a watershed moment in your path, a celebration of uniqueness and a reclaiming of personal authority. Just like a butterfly releases its chrysalis to expose its vivid wings, you may also remove the layers of training and conformity to reveal your genuine self.

Discovering your passions and purpose is an exhilarating trip into the depths of your spirit to unearth the ambitions and goals that ignite your heart. It's about discovering the hobbies that make you happy, the causes that pique your interest, and the skills that set you apart.

Begin by reminiscing about your childhood. Which activities did you appreciate the most? What were you naturally attracted to? What caused time to stand still? Often, our passions are latent inside us, waiting to be reawakened.

Consider the things that cause you to lose track of time, the activities in which you participate easily and with pure satisfaction. These might include painting, writing, hiking, and volunteering.

To further explore your interests, undertake the following activity.

- Make a "passion list": Make a list of all the activities, hobbies, and interests that pique your interest or make you happy. Do not restrain yourself; let your imagination run wild.

- Try new things: Step out of your comfort zone and attempt new hobbies that you've always been interested in. You could find secret abilities or hobbies you didn't know existed.

- Monitor your energy levels: Consider how you feel as you participate in various activities. Are you feeling vibrant and lively, or spent and depleted? Your body's reaction might reveal important indications about what actually excites you.

- Discovering your mission entails determining the distinctive contribution you wish to give to the world. It's about finding purpose and satisfaction in your life's job. To find your mission, ask yourself:

- What are your essential values? Which ideals are the most important to you?

- What issues are most important to me? What injustices or obstacles fuel your desire for change?

- What are my particular abilities and talents? What talents and abilities can you provide to the world?

Your mission does not have to be big or world-changing. It might be as easy as raising loving and sensitive children, creating beauty through art, or using your own experiences to help others recover. The idea is to discover something that speaks to your soul and gives your life significance.

Once you've identified your interests and purpose, it's crucial to connect your life with those principles. This entails making decisions that represent your basic values and objectives. It entails declaring "enough" to activities, relationships, or commitments that deplete your energy or undermine your integrity.

Begin by recognizing the areas of your life that do not correspond with your beliefs. Are you devoting too much time to work and ignoring your personal relationships? Are you pursuing ambitions that do not completely align with your heart? Do you sacrifice your ideals for the sake of acceptance or financial gain?

Once you've discovered the areas that want improvement, begin making tiny improvements. It might be as easy as making extra time for self-care, pursuing a passion project, or having an open discussion with a loved one about your needs.

Self-expression and creativity are very effective instruments for empowerment. When you express yourself truly, you connect with your inner power and knowledge. You express your own opinion and contribute to the world.

Creativity may take several forms. It might be writing, painting, dancing, singing, cooking, gardening, or any other activity in which you can express your own voice and vision.

Don't be scared to experiment with diverse modes of self-expression. The goal is to identify what speaks to you and provides you delight.

Discover Your Passions and Purpose

The path to accepting your true self starts with a search for your interests and purpose. This process is similar to uncovering hidden treasures buried behind layers of society expectations and self-doubt. It entails rediscovering the hobbies, interests, and causes that kindle a flame inside you.

Discovering your interests involves reconnecting with the activities that offer you pleasure, contentment, and a feeling of purpose. It's all about figuring out what makes time fly by, what activities make you feel invigorated and alive. These interests might range from writing, music, or dancing to volunteering, traveling, or establishing a company.

Your mission, on the other hand, is to discover meaning and importance in your life's work. It's about determining your distinctive contribution to the world and the legacy you wish to leave behind. This might be as easy as raising a loving family, contributing to your community, or utilizing your skills to inspire and encourage others.

Discovering your interests and purpose is a continuous journey of self-discovery and inquiry. It needs you to be open to new experiences, to listen to your intuition, and to believe in your own inner knowledge.

Begin by asking yourself a few basic questions:

- What hobbies make me feel most alive?
- What are my natural strengths?
- What topics do I like learning about?
- What issues or causes are most important to me?
- What influence do I want to have on the world?

The answers to these questions might provide important information about your interests and purpose. Never be scared to explore and try new things. The voyage of self-discovery is fraught with shocks and unexpected twists.

Remember that your interests and purpose are unique to you. There are no right or incorrect answers. The most essential thing is to discover something that speaks to your spirit and gives your life significance. By embracing your hobbies and connecting your life with your purpose, you may live a life that is both rewarding and meaningful.

Living a Life Consistent with Your Values

Aligning your life with your principles is a transforming process that involves both contemplation and action. It's about recognizing the differences between your present reality and your intended state, and then taking deliberate actions to close that gap.

The process starts with self-reflection. Take some time to reflect on your basic values, the guiding principles that shape who you are and what you stand for. Are your present decisions and activities consistent with these values? Are you living a life that represents your true self, or are you sacrificing your integrity in pursuit of external recognition or cultural expectations?

Once you've recognized the areas of misalignment, it's time to act. This might include making tough decisions, establishing boundaries, or venturing beyond of your comfort zone. It may include saying "enough" to relationships or activities that no longer serve you, while saying "yes" to possibilities that correspond with your interests and goals.

Aligning your life with your principles does not imply perfection. It's about making mindful decisions that get you closer to the life you want for yourself. It is about living with integrity, sincerity, and a strong sense of purpose.

Remember that every decision you make is a vote for the person you want to become. Aligning your activities with your principles allows you to have a satisfying and meaningful life. You claim your power, accept your real self, and cause a ripple effect of good change in the world.

Self-Reflection Questions:

1. What hobbies did you like and find fulfilling as a child? Consider the games you played, the hobbies you pursued, and the topics that piqued your attention.
2. What activities do you find easy and enjoyable? These might include artistic endeavors, intellectual difficulties, athletic activities, or social contacts.
3. Describe your key values. Which ideas and beliefs are the most important to you? Are your behaviors and decisions consistent with these values?

4. What issues or topics are you passionate about? Are there any injustices or difficulties that you are particularly enthusiastic about addressing?

5. Describe your particular qualities and abilities. How can you utilize your talents and abilities to positively influence the world?

Transformative Exercises:

1. Create a letter to your future self, imagining yourself enjoying a fulfilling life based on your beliefs and purpose in five years. Write a letter to your future self, outlining your achievements, struggles, and goals.

Transformative Exercise: Letter to Your Future Self

Objective: This exercise aims to help you envision your ideal future and reflect on your goals, achievements, and the challenges you may face along the way. By writing a letter to your future self, you can solidify your beliefs, purpose, and aspirations, making it easier to stay focused and motivated.

Instructions:

1. Find a quiet place where you can write without distractions.

2. Reflect on your current beliefs, values, and purpose.

3. Imagine yourself five years into the future, living a fulfilling life.

4. Write a letter to your future self, detailing your achievements, struggles, and goals.

5. Be honest and specific about what you hope to accomplish and how you plan to overcome challenges.

Example Entry

Date: June 13, 2024

Dear Future Me,

As I sit down to write this letter, I am filled with hope and excitement for the future. Today, I want to reflect on my journey and imagine where I will be in five years.

Achievements: I am incredibly proud of the work I have done to help others lead healthier lives. Over the past five years, I have published two more cookbooks that have been well-received by both critics and readers. My books are now bestsellers, and they have made a significant impact on how people approach healthy eating.

In addition to my books, I have expanded my reach by launching an online nutrition coaching program. This platform has allowed me to connect with a global audience and offer personalized advice and support. I have also had the opportunity to speak at numerous wellness conferences, sharing my knowledge and inspiring others to prioritize their health.

Struggles: The journey has not been without its challenges. Building a successful business while maintaining a balanced personal life has been tough. There have been moments of self-doubt and times when I felt overwhelmed by the demands of my career. However, I have learned to navigate these struggles by staying true to my purpose and seeking support from my loved ones.

Goals: Looking ahead, I have set several ambitious goals for myself. I plan to open a wellness center where people can come to learn about nutrition, participate in cooking classes, and engage in holistic health practices. I also aim to start a podcast to reach even more people and share stories of transformation and resilience.

On a personal level, I want to continue growing and learning. I hope to complete a yoga teacher training course to deepen my understanding of mind-body connection and incorporate more mindfulness practices into my daily life. Additionally, I am committed to maintaining strong relationships with my family and friends, as they are my greatest source of support and joy.

Final Thoughts: As I envision this future, I am filled with gratitude for the journey I am on. I know that there will be ups and downs, but I am confident that by staying focused on my beliefs and purpose, I will achieve my dreams. Future Sophie, I hope you are proud of the progress you have made and continue to inspire others with your passion and dedication.

With love and determination,

(Name)

Your Turn

Date:

Dear Future [Your Name],

Achievements:

Struggles:

Goals:

Final Thoughts:

With love and determination,

[Your Name]

Puzzle Exercise

Instruction:

Find the hidden words in the puzzle. Words can be written horizontally, vertically, or diagonally, forward or backward. Circle each word you find.

At the end of your attempt, check the Answer table to find out how correct you are.

Discovering and Living Your True Self

```
            S E L F - E X P R E S S I O N
M Z N T L G D W A A U T H E N T I C J L D E
M Y B Y F E N T Z A Z L C W Y K B P U W M J
R V T M R D M S J S A Z F T U N O U X X C Y
A Q W Q W L Z P K X B E L I E F S R W N W B
C V I S I O N E O X B M I S L L K P R U M E
A Z B G I I R K M W W E S X L L T O I C S V
F H M G G I N T E R E S T S F N M S T R T Q
Y U W S B F E M H S L R E O M V R E I E R K
T B O D J X J G L I L I M I S S I O N A E R
D R E F L E C T I O N L P E Y D O H G T N Q
J B G K P H E I R A E E A T N X G Z O I G X
T E R C D T O N K K S K S B T T N O P V T H
V L P D I V A L U E S M S S H Y B F J I H N
N B R P N E Y X E A C H I E V E M E N T S N
Q M S A E W D O D L D H O B B I E S Q Y K O
Y T L S J E C O E A X J N T L F I Q S C I V
D K I B O U N D A R I E S H K V N B X K X R
```

Achievements	**Passions**
Authentic	**Purpose**
Boundaries	**Reflection**
Beliefs	**Self-expression**
Creativity	**Strengths**
Empowerment	**Values**
Fulfillment	**Vision**
Hobbies	**Wellness**
Interests	**Worthiness**
Mission	**Writing**

Chapter 12: Thriving Beyond "Enough"

Saying "enough" is not the conclusion of the tale; rather, it is the beginning of a brave new chapter full of limitless possibilities and a renewed feeling of freedom. Imagine a life free of the weight of toxic relationships, where your energy is no longer sapped by emotional vampires, and your days are filled with pleasure, purpose, and genuine connections. This is the life that awaits you beyond "enough," one in which you flourish rather than just endure.

Consider a world in which you wake up every morning feeling invigorated and enthused about the day ahead. You surround yourself with people who encourage and motivate you, celebrate your accomplishments, and help you overcome obstacles. Your relationships are built on mutual respect, trust, and real love, not manipulation, guilt, or fear.

Your days are packed with things that feed your spirit and rekindle your interests. You pursue your ambitions with unflinching tenacity, believing that you deserve success and happiness. You put your well-being first, making time for self-care and nourishing your mind, body, and soul.

This vision may seem to be a faraway dream, particularly if you've been locked in a cycle of poisonous relationships for years. But it's within grasp. By expressing "enough" and reclaiming your authority, you've already taken the first step toward a better future.

Building resilience and fostering inner strength are critical to flourishing beyond "enough." Resilience is the capacity to recover from hardship, adapt to change, and retain a good attitude in the face of adversity. Inner strength is what permits us to withstand life's storms and come out stronger on the other side.

To create resilience, it is critical to establish appropriate coping skills for stress and adversity. This might include practicing mindfulness, getting regular exercise, spending time in nature, or building a supportive social network.

It's also important to confront negative thinking habits and create a good attitude. When confronted with setbacks or problems, concentrate on what you can control and take decisive action to handle the issue. Remind yourself of your strengths, previous triumphs, and accessible resources.

Cultivating inner strength entails establishing a strong feeling of self-worth and belief. It is about acknowledging your intrinsic worth as a human being, regardless of your circumstances or accomplishments. It is about embracing your flaws and accepting yourself completely, with all of your talents and failings.

Self-compassion may help you develop inner strength. Treat yourself with care and empathy, particularly if you are suffering. Forgive yourself for your faults and concentrate on learning and improving from them.

Surround yourself with good influences, individuals who encourage and inspire you. Reduce your exposure to negativity, whether from toxic individuals, social media, or the news.

Remember, developing resilience and inner strength is a continuous process. It requires time, effort, and dedication. However, the advantages are tremendous. When you are resilient and strong, you are better prepared to face life's problems, follow your aspirations, and live a really full life.

Many people have overcome hardship and prospered, and their tales serve as sources of hope and inspiration. No matter how tough our circumstances seem, we have the ability to overcome them and live a life of pleasure, purpose, and meaning. We may prosper beyond our wildest expectations by declaring "enough" to toxic relationships, developing resilience, and embracing our real selves.

Creating A Vision for Your Future

With the weight of toxic relationships removed off your shoulders, it's time to dream anew. Imagine a blank canvas on which you might paint a bright image of your future. What are you seeing? What is your desire? This is your chance to design a life that matches your own beliefs, interests, and goals.

You, too, can build a future full with pleasure, purpose, and satisfaction. Begin by identifying your dreams and aspirations. What have you always wanted to undertake but were held back by fear or self-doubt? What gives you delight and makes you feel alive? Write down your dreams, no matter how huge or tiny they may seem.

Next, make a vision board or write a strategy for your future. This is a concrete depiction of your goals, a reminder of what you're striving for. Fill it with photos, phrases, and affirmations that inspire and align with your goal.

When planning your future, examine the following questions:

- What sort of connections do you want to cultivate?
- What hobbies do you wish to pursue?
- What influence do you want to make on the world?

- What type of person do you aspire to become?

Remember that your vision is not fixed in stone. It may develop and alter as you mature and find new interests and opportunities. The goal is to have a clear direction, a guiding light that lights the route ahead.

By developing a vision for your future, you unleash a strong force of transformation. You give yourself permission to dream, hope, and believe in a greater future. You tap into your creativity and potential, setting the road for an incredible existence.

Developing Resilience and Inner Strength

Imagine resilience as a muscle that strengthens with each difficulty you conquer. Just as physical activity builds your body, hardship may strengthen your soul, instilling an inner resilience that helps you to weather life's storms with grace and resolve.

Resilience is not about avoiding suffering or pretending everything is OK. It's about admitting your grief, learning from it, and utilizing it as fuel for progress. It is about finding the strength to get back up after a fall, brush yourself off, and start going ahead.

Here are some basic techniques to develop resilience:

- Prioritize self-care: Take care of both your bodily and emotional needs. Eat nutritious meals, get adequate sleep, exercise on a regular basis, and do things you like.

- Establish a support system: Surround yourself with positive individuals who believe in you and promote your progress. Speak with a therapist, join a support group, or just tell a trusted friend or family member.

- Challenge negative thoughts: Don't allow setbacks or problems overwhelm you. Instead, concentrate on your abilities, previous accomplishments, and accessible resources.

- Set reasonable objectives. Break down big ambitions into smaller, more doable stages. Celebrate your success along the road, and don't be hesitant to seek assistance when you need it.

- Learn from your errors: We all make mistakes. Instead of obsessing on your shortcomings, see them as learning opportunities. Ask yourself, "What can I learn from this?" "How can I do better next time?"

Remember that resilience is not something you either have or do not have. It's a talent that may be honed and enhanced over time. You may create the inner strength and resilience required to flourish beyond "enough" by taking care of yourself, creating a strong support system, confronting negative beliefs, establishing realistic objectives, and learning from your failures.

Self-Reflection Questions:

1. What does flourish beyond "enough" mean for you? What are your future goals, hopes, and dreams?
2. What efforts have you made to reclaim your power and build a better future? What problems have you conquered, and what lessons have you learnt from them?
3. Describe your key values. Are your present decisions and activities in line with these values? If not, how can you make adjustments to have a more true and satisfying life?
4. Describe your strengths and shortcomings. How can you use your strengths and address your deficiencies to increase your resilience and inner strength?
5. What negative mental patterns should you challenge? What positive affirmations may help you develop a more hopeful and empowered mindset?

Transformative Exercises:

1. Practice thankfulness. Every day, list three things you're thankful for. This simple technique might help you change your emphasis from negativity to optimism and develop a more cheerful mindset.

Transformative Exercise: Practice Thankfulness

Developing a habit of thankfulness can significantly enhance your outlook on life, shifting your focus from negativity to positivity. By taking a few moments each day to reflect on and list three things you are grateful for, you can cultivate a more cheerful and optimistic mindset. This simple yet powerful exercise can have a transformative effect on your mental well-being.

How to Practice Thankfulness:

1. **Set Aside Time Daily**: Choose a specific time each day to practice thankfulness. This could be in the morning to start your day on a positive note or in the evening to reflect on the day's events.

2. **Find a Quiet Space**: Select a peaceful spot where you can sit quietly without distractions. This will help you focus on your thoughts and feelings.

3. **Reflect on Your Day**: Think about the events, people, or experiences that made a positive impact on your day.

4. **Write Down Three Things**: List three things you are thankful for. These can be big or small, as long as they bring you a sense of gratitude.

Example Entry:

Date: June 13, 2024

1. **Family Dinner**: I am thankful for the delicious dinner I shared with my family tonight. It was a wonderful opportunity to connect and enjoy each other's company.

2. **Morning Walk**: I am grateful for the peaceful morning walk I took today. The fresh air and beautiful scenery helped me start my day with a clear mind.

3. **Supportive Friend**: I appreciate my friend Sarah for her supportive and encouraging words today. She always knows how to lift my spirits.

Your Entry:

Puzzle Exercise

Instruction:

Find the hidden words in the puzzle. Words can be written horizontally, vertically, or diagonally, forward or backward. Circle each word you find.

At the end of your attempt, check the Answer table to find out how correct you are.

Flourishing After Toxic Relationships

```
            J F C Y S S B H Y H Q M W U S
B H G R A T I T U D E Y K Y E Q U Z V H R A
H Q A U T H E N T I C I T Y W V K I R T C Y
K J U A O L S U U L I D L A N N K A F P D D
K A A Z H L V B R N C Z Y J N A E D W S C I
G A W J S X W W E L L N E S S Q I H R U Z I
M E Y U E M P O W E R M E N T Z J T I P B G
A W S X L S T R E N G T H F D M R Z T P N G
W C H W F D O T R A N S F O R M A T I O N R
D C R C - N C H W E L L - B E I N G N R F Q
U A O O C Q L I C O M P A S S I O N G T C W
I K H Y A D T N E G A T I V I T Y J Y J U T
M J W C R V R E M I N D F U L N E S S L S P
Y O Y J E Q I S S P I M O T I V A T I O N M
C L A D V E R S I T Y W C R E A T I V I T Y
U U G Z M V P N I N N E R K N S T S T I T H
Y Y X C Y V D H J O A R G O C K X V Y X Y R
C X P V W F F G V F N Q H Y E H K N F I X Z
```

Adversity	Negativity
Authenticity	Resilience
Compassion	Self-Care
Creativity	Support
Empowerment	Transformation
Future	Vision
Gratitude	Well-being
Inner Strength	Wellness
Mindfulness	Worthiness
Motivation	Writing

Conclusion

Enough resonates through the depths of your heart, creating a symphony of emancipation and fresh strength. You've descended into the depths of poisonous relationships, addressed the darkness of your history, and risen with a tenacity that outshines any challenge.

My vivacious vitality, dulled by the creeping poison of poisonous love and I was able to change as I recovered her authority, established healthy boundaries, and let go of a love that no longer served me.

My experience demonstrates the transforming power of declaring enough. It's a statement that you'll no longer accept disrespect, manipulation, or negligence. It is a commitment to upholding your beliefs, safeguarding your well-being, and living a life that is authentic to yourself.

As you approach a fresh beginning, remember that expressing enough is a never-ending process of self-discovery and progress. It's a commitment to prioritizing your health, establishing healthy boundaries, and cultivating soulful connections. It's about being true to yourself, following your interests, and having a satisfying and meaningful life.

When you say enough, its power is not in the word itself, but in the deeds it inspires. It takes strength to leave bad relationships, tenacity to endure hardship, and discernment to select a career that respects your real self. It's the calm power that comes from recognizing your value and refusing to accept less than you deserve.

So, let the echoes of enough to resound inside you, directing you to a future full of love, pleasure, and boundless possibilities. Accept the power of this simple yet transformational phrase, and watch your life blossom in ways you never imagined imaginable.

ANSWER KEY

w1

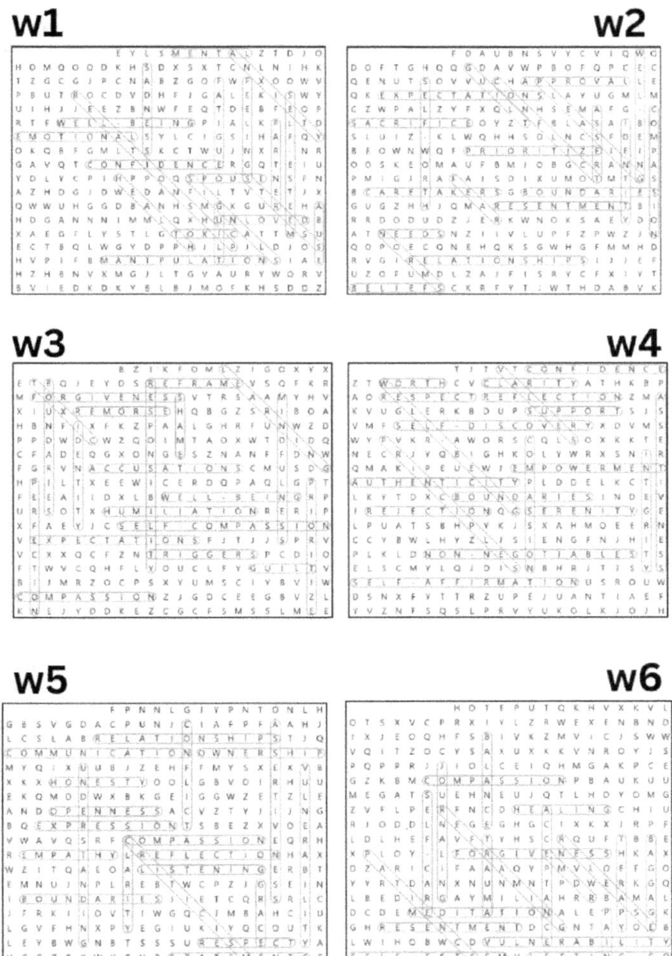

w2

w3

w4

w5

w6

ANSWER KEY

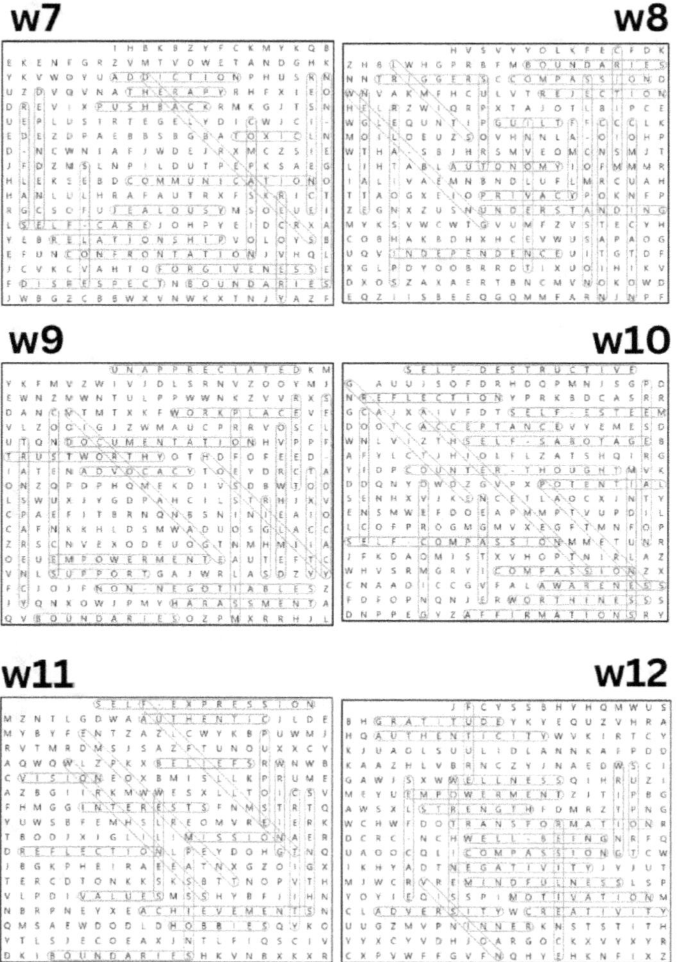

w7

w8

w9

w10

w11

w12